The judiciary in the magistrates' courts

Rod Morgan (University of Bristol) and Neil Russell (RSGB)

Prepared for:

The Home Office
50 Queen Anne's Gate
London SW1H 9AT

The Lord Chancellor's Department
54-60 Victoria Street
London SW1E 4QW

Additional copies of this report can be obtained from:

RDS
Communications Development Unit
Room 201
Home Office
50 Queen Anne's Gate
London SW1H 9AT

Tel. 020 7273 2084

ISBN 1 84082 574 x

ACKNOWLEDGEMENTS

Any research project involving fieldwork is a team effort. This project was especially complicated and its completion on time depended on not just the helpfulness but the considerable effort and enthusiastic co-operation of a very large number of people within the ten courts from which we collected most of our data, within the two government departments (the Lord Chancellor's Department (LCD) and the Home Office) who assisted and oversaw our efforts, and within the three research organisations involved (The University of Bristol, Research Surveys of Great Britain (RSGB) and CRG). We cannot thank everyone individually and it would be invidious to try. We should name those persons, however, who were particularly important in putting together this report and offering guidance throughout its production.

At the University of Bristol, Lee Maitland acted as our central co-ordinator for data collection and liaised throughout with the staff at the ten courts which participated in the study. Her commitment and attention to detail was vital. Colleagues Gwynn Davis, Andrew Sanders and Julie Vennard gave valuable advice both with regard to early planning and the final report. Within RSGB, our especial thanks go to Katharine Davis who steered through much of the data analysis and to Tony Fricker, Alison MacDonald and Matthew Tassier who worked tirelessly to tabulate the quantitative data on which much of this report is based. In the RSGB team thanks must also go to Cynthia Pinto who was a constant source of wise advice and to Bill Blyth whose statistical expertise and measured assurance that we could accomplish what seemed at times to be an impossibly complex task was both inspirational and necessary. Chapter Five of this report, on the cost implications of what we have found, was drafted by Richard Gaunt of CRG without whose expertise our conclusions would be lacking an essential dimension. Many other colleagues assisted at various times.

We thank Dr Hans-Jurgen Bartsch of the Directorate of Legal Affairs at the Council of Europe, Strasbourg, for sending out our questionnaire regarding lay involvement in judicial decision-making in Council of Europe member states. That exercise greatly broadened our knowledge of arrangements elsewhere.

We should also give substantial credit to our team of court observers who worked with great enthusiasm initially in understanding what we were attempting to achieve, assisting in the final development phase of the data collection materials and finally conducting the observations with a remarkable level of thoroughness and efficiency.

We reported regularly to the Home Office and LCD via a steering committee chaired by Mark Ormerod. We are grateful to him and his colleagues for both their support and wise advice when technical difficulties were encountered and when the confidence of some of the many magistrates and court staff who have assisted us was endangered by provocative newspaper articles suggesting that the research was being steered by conclusions already decided. It was not so, but that message needed skilfully to be reiterated. All communications were via our Home Office liaison officer, initially Jennifer Airs and subsequently Catriona Mirrlees-Black and Rachel Pennant. We thank them for dealing with our many requests without delay.

Finally, our thanks to the literally hundreds of magistrates and magistrates' courts' staff and practitioners who attended meetings to listen to our research plans, who have subsequently answered our questions, completed our diaries and been willing to have their daily work observed and reported on. We hope we have not let them down: the criminal justice system in England and

Wales depends crucially on their commitment and sense of justice. We hope that this report will ensure that whatever public debate now takes place about the future of the magistrates' courts is better informed than it would otherwise have been.

Rod Morgan, University of Bristol
Neil Russell, RSGB

CONTENTS

SUMMARY

This research was jointly commissioned by the Lord Chancellor's Department and the Home Office. The study was undertaken during the first nine months of 2000 by a research team comprising the University of Bristol and two commercial companies, RSGB (a division of Taylor Nelson Sofres plc) and CRG, Cardiff, specialists in market research and cost benefit analysis respectively.

Lay magistrates sit part time and are not paid for their services. They are selected for appointment on the basis of six key qualities: good character, understanding and communication, social awareness, maturity and sound temperament, sound judgement and commitment. They deal with criminal matters in the adult and youth courts and with civil matters, particularly family matters in the Family Court. Magistrates who are members of specialist committees are responsible for the administration of the liquor licensing system and for the grant or refusal of applications for licences or permits relating to betting and the registration of gaming clubs. Lay magistrates are advised on legal points by a professionally qualified legal advisor.

Stipendiary magistrates sit full time and are legally qualified members of the professional judiciary (they must be solicitors or barristers). They undertake the same range of criminal and civil work as lay magistrates but are often assigned to deal with cases which are likely to be lengthy or particularly complex. There are also part time or acting stipendiary magistrates who are similarly legally qualified. Since August 2000 stipendiary magistrates have borne the title District Judge (Magistrates' Courts), in recognition of their membership of the professional judiciary, but in this report they are referred to by the more familiar title.

Purposes of the research

The research was commissioned to:

- investigate the present balance of lay and stipendiary magistrates and the arguments supporting this balance
- test the weight and validity of these arguments
- consider whether each type of magistrate is deployed in the most effective way.

Existing arguments for and against lay and stipendiary magistrates can be summarised as:

- participatory democracy and justice versus consistency and the rule of law
- local justice versus national consistency
- open versus case-hardened minds
- symbolic legitimacy versus effectiveness and efficiency
- cost – high or low.

Methodology

The research comprised seven types of data collection:

- baseline information on the budgets, buildings, court staff and magistrates' characteristics. Data were gathered both nationally and locally, and included information on ten magistrates' courts in London and the provinces, with and without stipendiaries
- 2,019 self-completed magistrates' diaries, spanning three-week sessions, covering activities, timings etc. from the ten courts
- 1,120 self-completed magistrates' questionnaires addressing issues of sitting arrangements, their views on balance between lay and stipendiaries etc. from the ten courts
- observations of 535 court sessions at the ten courts
- 400 telephone interviews with regular court users from the ten courts
- public opinion survey: conducted with a nationally representative sample of 1,753 members of public
- 23 responses to a letter to representatives of the Council of Europe member states.

Composition and working practices of the magistracy

Composition

At the time of the research the magistracy comprised:

- approximately 30,400 lay magistrates
- 96 full-time stipendiaries
- 146 part-time stipendiaries.

The lay magistracy:

- is gender balanced
- is ethnically representative of the population at a national level
- is overwhelmingly drawn from professional and managerial ranks
- comprises a high proportion (two-fifths) who have retired from full-time employment.

In comparison, stipendiaries:

- are mostly male and white
- tend to be younger.

Sitting patterns

Lay magistrates:

- sit in court an average 41.4 occasions annually (although many sit a good deal more frequently)
- devote (taking holidays into account) an extended morning or afternoon to the post once a week
- additionally spend the equivalent, on average, of a full working week on training and other duties.

The contracts of full-time stipendiaries require them to perform judicial duties five days a week, 44 weeks of the year. However there is some ambiguity as to what this means in terms of court sittings. Provincial stipendiaries sit more often than their colleagues do in London, but both groups sit in court closer to four days per week.

Lay magistrates usually sit in panels of three, but sometimes of two (16% of observed panels). Stipendiaries nearly always sit alone but on rare occasions sit together with lay magistrates.

Caseload allocation

While stipendiaries take on more or less the full range of cases and appearances, they tend to be allocated more complex, prolonged and sensitive cases. Unlike lay magistrates, their time is concentrated on triable-either-way rather than summary cases.

Working methods and decision-making

Speed

Stipendiary magistrates deal with all categories of cases and appearances more quickly than their lay colleagues because they retire from court sessions less often and more briefly (0.2 compared to 1.2 occasions per session, for only 3 compared to 16 minutes). They also deal with cases more quickly on average (9 minutes compared to 10 minutes). This means:

- stipendiaries hear 22 per cent more appearances than lay magistrates per standardised court session (12.2 compared to 10)
- if stipendiaries were allocated an identical caseload to lay magistrates, it is estimated that they would deal with 30 per cent more appearances.

The greater speed of stipendiaries is not achieved at the expense of inquisition and challenge; on the contrary, hearings before stipendiaries typically involve more questions being asked and more challenges being made.

Manner of working: adjournments and bail

Both lay and stipendiary magistrates are invariably judged to meet high standards in dealing with court business (attentiveness, clarity of pronouncements, courtesy, and so on). However, stipendiaries are considered to perform better in relation to those criteria that suggest greater confidence – showing command over the proceedings and challenging parties responsible for delay.

Fewer appearances before stipendiaries lead to adjournments (45% compared to 52%). This is partly because fewer applications are made to stipendiaries but also because they are more likely to resist applications for adjournments (97% compared to 93%). It is therefore likely that the employment of additional stipendiaries would lead to fewer court appearances overall.

Lay magistrates are less likely to:

- refuse defendants bail in cases where the prosecution seeks custody and the defence applies for bail (19% compared to 37%)
- make use of immediate custody as a sentence (12% of triable-either-way cases compared to 25%).

The employment of additional stipendiaries might therefore significantly increase the prison population.

Stipendiaries tend to run their courts themselves and rely very little on their court legal advisors when it comes to making and explaining decisions and announcements. This calls into question whether they need legally qualified court advisors.

The views of regular court practitioners

A sample of 400 court practitioners (court advisors, solicitors, CPS personnel, probation officers) were surveyed by telephone.

Very few court users expressed 'no' or only 'a little' confidence in either type of magistrate, but stipendiaries were more likely to inspire a 'great deal' or a 'lot' of confidence. Users found it harder to generalise about lay magistrates, indicating a greater range in their performance.

The court users expressed very similar views to the court observers when asked to rate dimensions of behaviour. Stipendiaries were widely seen as:

- more efficient, more consistent and more confident in their decision-making
- questioning defence lawyers appropriately
- giving clear reasons for decisions
- showing command over proceedings.

Lay magistrates were more often judged better at:

- showing courtesy to defendants and other court members
- using simple language
- showing concern to distressed victims.

But the majority of respondents did not think lay and stipendiary magistrates differed on these criteria.

Regular court practitioners, particularly lawyers and CPS personnel, said that they and their colleagues behave differently when appearing before lay and stipendiary magistrates. They:

- prepare better for stipendiaries
- try to be more precise and concise in their statements to them
- anticipate that they will be questioned and challenged more.

Court legal advisors on the other hand said that they prepare more for lay magistrates, because they anticipate the need to give legal advice to them.

Public opinions of the magistracy

A nationally representative sample of 1,753 members of the public were interviewed regarding their views on, and knowledge of the magistracy.

Whereas the overwhelming majority of the public is aware of the terms 'magistrate' and 'magistrates' court', only a minority have heard of 'lay' as opposed to 'stipendiary' magistrates.

When the difference between them is explained, almost three-quarters (73%) say that they were not aware of this difference.

Only a bare majority of respondents correctly identify that most criminal cases are dealt with in the magistrates' courts, and that juries do not make decisions there. Knowledge about the qualifications and sitting practices of lay magistrates is even less accurate. Respondents who are more knowledgeable about the system tend to have greater confidence in it.

Having had the differences explained to them, most of the public thinks that:

- lay magistrates represent the views of the community better than stipendiaries (63% compared to 9% - the remaining 28% see no difference or don't know)
- lay magistrates are more likely to be sympathetic to defendants' circumstances (41% compared to 12%)
- stipendiaries are better at making correct judgements of guilt or innocence (36% compared to 11%) and managing court business effectively (48% compared to 9%)
- there is no difference between lay and stipendiaries in awareness of the effect of crimes on victims and approaching each case afresh.

In addition, when comparing single magistrates with panels:

- a small majority of respondents (53%) consider that motoring offences are suitable to be heard by a single magistrate
- a large majority think that the more serious decisions of guilty/not guilty (74%) and sending to prison (76%) should be decided by panels of magistrates.

Most respondents think that the work of the magistrates' courts should be divided equally between the two types of magistrates, or that the type of magistrate does not matter.

The direct and indirect costs of lay and stipendiary magistrates

If only directly attributable costs (salaries, expenses, training) are considered, lay magistrates are much cheaper because they are not paid directly and many do not claim loss of earnings. A sizeable minority does not even claim their allowable travelling expenses. A lay magistrate costs on average £495 per annum compared to the £90,000 per annum total employment costs of a stipendiary. These translate into a cost per appearance before lay and stipendiary magistrates of £3.59 and £20.96 respectively (Table 1). When indirect costs (premises, administration staff, etc.) are brought into the equation the gap between the two groups narrows, to £52.10 and £61.78.

Table 1

The cost of appearing before lay and stipendiary magistrates (per appearance)

	Lay Magistrates	Stipendiary Magistrates
	£	£
Direct costs (salary, expenses, training)	3.59	20.96
Indirect costs (premises, administration staff etc.)	48.51	40.82
Direct & indirect costs	52.10	61.78

The effect upon costs of substituting stipendiary for lay magistrates

There would have to be a significant increase in the use of the more productive stipendiaries to enable administrative staff and courtroom reductions to be made on any scale.

If blocks of work currently undertaken by lay magistrates were transferred to stipendiaries:

- one stipendiary would be needed for every 30 magistrates, if all lay tribunals comprised three justices
- one for every 28, if the present proportion of tribunals comprising only two lay justices were to continue.

Stipendiaries' greater tendency to resist adjournments and their greater use of custody at the pre-trial and sentencing stages means that if the number of stipendiaries were doubled (assuming present patterns were retained):

- there would be a reduction of 10,270 appearances in connection with indictable offences, giving an additional cost of £0.88 million per annum (a net increase because the reduced rates of adjournments do not overcome the higher attributable costs of stipendiaries)
- the number of remands in custody would increase by 6,200 per annum. Assuming an average remand period of 46 days, this has an associated cost of around £24 million (essentially falling on the Prison Service)
- the number of custodial sentences would increase by 2,760 per annum, costing £13.6 million. Set against this is the cost of the type of sentence that the offender would have received in the place of a prison sentence. If this is taken as some form of community penalty then the overall additional cost of this increase in custodial sentences would be around £8.5 million.

The effect upon costs of substituting lay for stipendiary magistrates

Alternatively if there were no stipendiaries, then there would be an increase in the number of appearances of 10,270, the number of remands in custody would decrease by 6,200, and the number of custodial sentences would decrease by 2,760 – with each of the consequent cost savings.

Other jurisdictions

Drawing on the 23 responses from the Council of Europe member states and enquiries to other (mostly Common Law) jurisdictions, it can be seen that there are three principal models of adjudication:

- the *professional*
- the *lay*
- the *hybrid* (mixed lay and professional).

Each of these can be refined in terms of whether decision-making is by single persons or panels, and the number of tiers into which criminal cases and courts are divided.

However there is no straightforward relationship between the degree to which democracy is embedded and lay involvement in judicial decision-making. Many longstanding democracies involve lay persons while others do not. The re-establishment of democracy in a country does not necessarily stimulate the introduction of lay involvement in judicial decision-making, sometimes the reverse occurs, depending on the cultural and political tradition.

The most common arrangements for lay involvement comprise lay persons making decisions in the lowest tier, or sitting alongside professional judges in the middle or higher tiers. However, it is also common that their decisions are restricted to minor non-imprisonable offences. More serious decisions are invariably made by professionals or hybrid panels.

England and Wales is the only jurisdiction identified in this research where such a high proportion of criminal cases, including serious cases, are decided by lay persons. In addition, the allocation of cases to either lay or stipendiary magistrates by chance, rather than by policy, is unique to this jurisdiction.

Conclusion

Though the research does not point in a particular policy direction, the findings do indicate how the public and court users are likely to react to certain proposals for change.

Although the public do not have strong feelings about the precise role of magistrates, they think that summary offences, particularly if not contested, can be dealt with by a single magistrate but that panels should make the more serious judicial decisions. Cost considerations suggest that this could only be achieved (in the short-term at least) by continuing to make extensive use of lay magistrates.

Criminal justice practitioners, while appreciative of the quality of service given by lay magistrates, have greater confidence in professional judges (stipendiaries). Furthermore governmental pressure to make the criminal courts more efficient, and to reduce the time that cases take to complete, will also tend to favour the greater efficiency of stipendiary magistrates. However, this has to be balanced against the potential increase in cost to the Prison Service.

The nature and balance of contributions made by lay and stipendiary magistrates could be altered to better satisfy these wider considerations, but should not prejudice the integrity and support of a system founded on strong traditions. Not only is the office of Justice of the Peace ancient and in an important tradition of voluntary public service, it is also a direct manifestation of government policy which encourages *active citizens* in an *active community*. In no other jurisdiction does the criminal court system depend so heavily on such voluntary unpaid effort. At no stage during the study was it suggested that in most respects the magistrates' courts do not work well or fail to command general confidence. It is our view, therefore, that eliminating or greatly diminishing the role of lay magistrates would not be widely understood or supported.

1   INTRODUCTION AND BACKGROUND

1.1   INTRODUCTION

This report is about the work of the magistrates' courts in England and Wales and a comparison of the contribution that lay and stipendiary magistrates make to the work of those courts. Lay magistrates sit part time and are not paid for their services. They are selected for appointment on the basis of six key qualities: good character, understanding and communication, social awareness, maturity and sound temperament, sound judgement and commitment. They deal with criminal matters in the Adult and Youth Courts and with civil matters, particularly in relation to family matters in the Family Court. Members of specialist committees are responsible for the administration of the liquor licensing system and for the grant or refusal of applications for licences or permits relating to betting and the registration of gaming clubs. Lay magistrates are advised on legal points by a professionally qualified legal advisor.

Stipendiary magistrates sit full time and are legally qualified members of the professional judiciary (they must be solicitors or barristers). They undertake the same range of criminal and civil work as lay magistrates but are often assigned to deal with cases which are likely to be lengthy or particularly complex. There are also part time or acting stipendiary magistrates who are similarly legally qualified.[1]

The work was commissioned jointly by the Lord Chancellor's Department, which is responsible for the administration of the Magistrates' Courts Service, and the Home Office. The research was conducted in the first half of 2000 and should contribute to the broad debate which is taking place about the future of the magistrates' courts within our criminal court system. This first chapter outlines the broad framework within which the research was conducted, sets out the questions we were asked to address and summarises the data collection methods that we employed.

Criminal court systems are generally divided into two or more tiers so as to reserve to the upper tier or tiers those cases regarded as relatively grave. For these cases the higher courts alone can impose the most severe penalties. Because of the relative gravity of their business the higher courts often employ procedures more elaborate, and thus expensive, than those in the lower courts. These more elaborate procedures are generally held to provide safeguards commensurate with the gravity of the cases being dealt with and the likely penalties which will be imposed should the cases be proved. The higher courts generally deal with only a small minority of cases and in many jurisdictions one of the distinctions between the different court tiers concerns the involvement of lay persons, either as jurors, assessors or part-time magistrates, in decision-making.

In neither of these respects is the criminal court system in England and Wales unusual. The English system has two tiers, the magistrates' courts and the Crown Court. The magistrates' courts, the lower tier, deal with the overwhelming majority – approximately 96 per cent – of criminal court business and magistrates' powers are generally limited to a maximum sentence of six months imprisonment. The two tiers involve distinct decision-making arrangements. In the magistrates' courts magistrates decide both matters of fact and sentence. In the Crown Court all matters of fact are decided by a jury and sentences are determined by judges. What is unusual about the English system is that lay persons play so important a role at *both* levels. In the Crown Court the jurors are lay persons for whom participation, generally over two weeks, is normally a once-in-a-lifetime

---

[1] Part-time stipendiary magistrates are guaranteed a minimum of 15 days court sittings per annum.

experience. In the magistrates' courts questions of fact and sentence are decided in the overwhelming majority of cases – we estimate 91 per cent – by lay magistrates, that is, unpaid volunteers who generally sit in court for half a day a week during judicial careers typically lasting ten to 20 years. It is this latter feature of the English and Welsh criminal court system – the reliance on lay magistrates in the lower courts – which most overseas visitors find remarkable and which appears not to be replicated in any other jurisdiction. It is the work of lay magistrates, and how it compares with their full-time lawyer colleagues – the stipendiary magistrates who we estimate deal with nine per cent of the criminal work of the magistrates' courts – which is the focus of this study.

Before setting out the questions this report aims to explore, it is necessary to say something about the policy trends which currently frame the work of the magistrates' courts, or will do so shortly.

1.2   POLICY TRENDS

The policy issue which has preoccupied many persons concerned with our criminal court system during the period in which the present study was conducted is the Government's intention to alter the method by which some cases are allocated between the magistrates' courts and the Crown Court. There are three classes of criminal offences in the English system. Between the summary offences that can be dealt with only in the magistrates' courts and the indictable offences that must be heard in the Crown Court is the very large number of offences that can go to either court – the so-called triable-either-way offences. Whereas hitherto any defendant charged with an either-way offence has been able to elect trial by jury, the Government proposes, following the recommendation of a Royal Commission (1993, Chapter Six, paragraphs 6-7) that henceforth the magistrates should decide on this issue. This proposition arguably does not raise any question of principle. There is not, and, contrary to popular belief, there never has been, a right to trial by jury (see Ashworth, 1998, 255-262) and over the years successive administrations have re-classified many criminal offences downwards to summary only (Darbyshire, 1997a). Nevertheless the Government's proposed legislation throws into sharper relief some questions which lie at the heart of the English and Welsh system. How is the quality of justice dispensed by the magistrates' courts generally regarded by defendants and the public? To what extent can lay magistrates be regarded as surrogate jurors, or might they be? And is it reasonable that defendants protesting their innocence who elect trial by jury should potentially be both tried and sentenced, not by a panel of lay magistrates, but by a stipendiary magistrate sitting alone?

At the time that we conducted this research there were approximately 30,400 part-time lay magistrates in England and Wales, 96 full-time professional or stipendiary magistrates and 146 part-time or acting stipendiary magistrates. For historical reasons there has always been a distinction between stipendiary magistrates in London and those appointed to provincial commissions. By the time this report is published stipendiary magistrates will, following the Access to Justice Act 1999, Schedule 11, have been re-titled district judges and their services integrated. However, district judge is as yet an unfamiliar title for stipendiaries and so we shall throughout this report refer to professional magistrates as stipendiaries.

The office of magistrate or Justice of the Peace can be traced back to the Statute of Westminster 1361 and is testament to the continuity of English institutions and their adaptation to changing circumstances (Milton, 1967; Moir, 1969; Skyrme, 1994). Until the early 19th century the justices of the peace were responsible for almost everything that today passes for local government as well as policing and justice. Their contemporary role is entirely judicial encompassing licensing, family and youth court work in addition to the adult criminal court. Lay magistrates are organised in benches and their administration has undergone substantial change in recent years. They are appointed by the Lord Chancellor to a Commission of the Peace and assigned to petty sessional areas (PSAs), which are in turn grouped into Magistrates' Court Committee areas (MCCs). A good deal of horizontal integration has been taking place and following the Police and Magistrates' Courts Act 1994 the administration of magistrates' courts has been centralised within MCCs. Through a process of amalgamation the number of PSAs and MCCs has been greatly reduced. Many small and little used courthouses, particularly in rural areas, have been closed. Instead of most PSAs having their own justices' clerk (the lay benches' chief legal advisor and court administrator), more and more have been grouped under a common justices' clerk and each MCC is now headed by a chief executive with overall administrative responsibility for the PSAs making up the area. This process of radical horizontal integration has not yet run its course. Whereas on 1 April 1 1999, there were 84 MCCs in England and Wales, the number is set to reduce to 42 by 2001 when the administrative structure for magistrates' courts will be coterminous with police authority, Crown Prosecution Service (CPS) and probation service boundaries. This process has necessarily been attended by strain. Benches have become much larger and some lay magistrates perceive their local community ties, status and support to have been eroded.

Stipendiary magistrates are of more recent origin (see Skyrme, 1994; Seago, Walker and Wall, 1995). They emerged in inner London in the first half of the 18th century in response to the increasing volume of court work and the questionable performance of some lay magistrates, notably the scandalous 'Trading Justices' in Middlesex. They were first officially recognised by the Middlesex Justices Act 1792.

Legislative provision for the appointment of stipendiaries in the provinces followed in the 19th century but was little acted on so that, until the 1970s, the appointment of stipendiaries remained a largely London phenomenon. Indeed until 1964 stipendiary magistrates exercised sole jurisdiction in inner London. In 1974 there were 39 stipendiaries in London and only 10 outside London. The Administration of Justice Act 1973 increased the permissible number of stipendiary appointments in the provinces to 40 and in London to 60, a higher threshold more acted on in the provinces (and since increased to 50) as court workloads, particularly in the metropolitan areas, increased and more complex and serious cases became triable summarily. At the time that we collected our data in spring 2000 there were 47 full-time stipendiaries in London and 49 in the provinces: there were a further 146 part-time stipendiaries nationally. It follows that the growth in the number of stipendiary magistrates has so far been modest (see Figure 1.1), proportionately no greater than the increase in the number of lay magistrate appointments made necessary in recent decades by the growth in magistrates' courts business. Nevertheless the balance in the contribution made by lay and stipendiary magistrates remains a sensitive issue.

The appointment of an additional stipendiary, particularly in a MCC area where there has not previously been one, typically encounters resistance from some lay colleagues who see it as marginalising their own position. This is particularly the case where the appointment originates not from a recommendation from the Lord Chancellor's Advisory Committee but from the recently established Magistrates' Courts Service Inspectorate (MCSI). Such interventions are taken by some lay magistrates to represent an aspect of excessive centralised administration and governmental managerialism.

Figure 1.1

Magistrates' courts, England and Wales: caseloads and magistrates

Year	Defendants proceeded against in magistrates' court (thousands)	Lay Magistrates	Stipendiary Magistrates
1971	1,796	19,250	45
1981	2,294	25,435	51
1991	1,985	29,062	68
1998	1,952	30,361	91
1999	1,884	30,308	96
2000	Not available	30,400 (estimated)	96

This reaction is scarcely surprising. Successive recent administrations have sought to achieve greater effectiveness and efficiency in the court service, in line with similar efforts made in relation to criminal justice agencies generally. In their reports on the magistrates' courts within MCC areas, the MCSI regularly comments on the number of sittings undertaken by lay magistrates and the need to manage court workloads more effectively. One of the present government's election pledges was to halve the time from arrest to sentence for persistent young offenders and, following publication of a White Paper (Home Office, 1997b), the Youth Justice Board was established to oversee local youth justice structures and monitor, among other things, the processing, including fast-tracking, of persistent young offenders coming before the youth court.

The MCSI has developed core performance measures (CPMs) for the measurement of court work (HMMCSI, 1999) and other recommendations from a Home Office review, the Narey Report on *Delay in the Criminal Justice System* (Home Office), have been implemented. So-called 'Narey Courts' and 'Narey hearings', 'early first hearings' (EFHs) involving abbreviated paperwork so as to fast-track straightforward guilty plea cases, and 'early administrative hearings' (EAHs) in cases where not guilty pleas are anticipated and where, shortly after charge, legal aid and other case management issues can ideally be speedily sorted out, have become part of the administrative parlance of magistrates' courts.

The Narey reforms have served to accelerate another trend with sensitive implications as far as many lay magistrates are concerned: the granting of powers to justices' clerks which were previously the prerogative of magistrates (see Darbyshire, 1999). EAHs can be conducted by single magistrates (which may mean a stipendiary) or by justices' clerks. The provision is the latest in a long line granting clerks powers previously reserved to magistrates, thereby arguably blurring the line between the judicial role of the magistrates and the administrative responsibilities of the clerk. Stipendiaries have also been empowered to act alone in the youth court whereas previously they were required to sit as panels, which necessarily meant their sitting with lay magistrates. Given that the horizontal integration of PSAs into common clerkships has meant that there are fewer justices' clerk posts, and that justices' clerks often serve as part-time stipendiary magistrates and become full-time stipendiaries (see Chapter Two), these developments are interpreted by some lay magistrates as the 'writing on the wall' for their office.

The joint commissioning by the Home Office and Lord Chancellor's Department (LCD) of the research of which this report is the product, and the establishment in December 1999 of a major review of the criminal court system led by a senior judge, Lord Justice Auld, has naturally fuelled these lay magistrate anxieties. The Government has emphasised that it is 'committed to the principle of the lay magistracy continuing to play a significant part in our system of justice' (the unpublished commissioning document jointly issued by the Home Office and Lord Chancellor's

Department for this research, paragraph 1.5). Yet the fact that this research is 'to assess the relative costs, effectiveness and other benefits/disadvantages of stipendiary and lay magistrates' in order to 'assess whether the current balance between the use of lay magistrates and stipendiaries is satisfactory' (*Ibid.*, paragraphs 1.5-1.6), and the fact that Lord Justice Auld's terms of reference include 'the structure and organisation of, and distribution of work between courts; (and) their composition, including the use of juries and of lay and stipendiary magistrates', has encouraged suspicions among many lay magistrates that there is a hidden agenda of change in which their future is unlikely to be advanced.

This is the policy climate in which we undertook our data collection and which explains the methodology we adopted. We have repeatedly emphasised to the lay and stipendiary magistrates and Magistrates' Courts Service staff who generously gave us their time in the undertaking of this research, that we knew of no hidden agenda and that if there was to be a public debate about the future composition of the magistrates' courts then it would best be served were we able to provide as full a picture of what magistrates do as we were able. The overwhelming co-operation we received suggests that this claim was generally accepted.

1.3 THE RESEARCH REMIT

We were asked to address the following specific issues:

- to describe the type of work done by lay and stipendiary magistrates
- to describe how the two groups process similar work (the time taken to deal with comparable business, the amount of advice required, their pattern of decision-making, and so on)
- to describe the sitting and listing arrangements for both groups
- to assess the quality of the decisions made by the two groups
- to assess the validity of certain commonly held views as to the merits and demerits of lay as opposed to stipendiary magistrates
- to assess the effects on the work of other criminal justice agencies of the manner in which the two groups undertake their work
- to assess the cost implications of employing the two groups and of changing their relative contribution
- to investigate what the public at large knows about the operation of the present system and what it sees as the benefits and disadvantages of it
- to investigate the views of regular court users (defence lawyers, CPS personnel, police and probation officers, Victim Support workers, and so on) about the performance of the two groups
- to describe the extent to which lay persons are involved in judicial decision-making in other jurisdictions.

Two aspects of this brief require elaboration, one briefly and the other at length.

First, we want to elaborate on the requirement that we consider the quality of magistrates' decision-making. Use of the word 'quality' gave rise to many questions at the bench meetings we held during the preliminary phase of the research and it is important that we should take this opportunity to emphasise what we do and what we do *not* take the term to mean and what we shall *not* be attempting to conclude in the report that follows. We were not in a position to assess the rectitude, appropriateness or justice of the decisions made by lay and stipendiary magistrates. We employed a corps of temporary fieldworkers to observe court proceedings (see Appendix B) and we did not think it appropriate to ask them to make such assessments, nor shall we attempt such an exercise on the basis of the data they collected. We shall report how decisions are made, and as part of that exercise, we asked our court observers to apply the same sort of standards that magistrates apply to each other for appraisal purposes – for example, whether announcements are made in non-jargon language, easy for defendants and witnesses to understand, and so on (see Appendix B). We also report the nature of magistrates' decisions. It is to some extent possible, therefore, to apply the test of consistency – as between lay and stipendiary magistrates, for example – an important criterion of quality when it comes to the rule of law. Further, we report the views that court users and the public at large form of magistrates, an indirect measure of quality. But it will be for our readers to determine whether one pattern of decisions is more appropriate than another.

The second issue concerns the requirement that we assess the validity of commonly held views as to the merits and demerits of employing lay and stipendiary magistrates. This is a fundamental question that requires extended preliminary examination as to the nature of these commonly held views.

1.4 GENERAL ARGUMENTS REGARDING LAY VERSUS STIPENDIARY MAGISTRATES

The commissioning document for this research set out 14 arguments, comments or observations regarding the alleged merits or disadvantages of employing lay versus stipendiary magistrates. The list was not exhaustive and though it mostly included viewpoints capable of evaluation – for example, 'that parties [to court] proceedings, particularly legal representatives, have more respect for stipendiaries and this influences their own behaviour on, for example, asking for adjournments' – such statements were placed alongside others – for example, 'that as volunteers magistrates are seen as an important example of the Government's support for the voluntary sector' – which is by definition true, but about which little more can be said except in the context of the brief account of democratic theory which follows.

We think that the commonly held views outlined in the commissioning document and others that we have identified can be grouped under five headings, as given below.

1.4.1 Participatory Democracy and 'Clapham Omnibus' Justice vs. Consistency and the Rule of Law

The lay magistracy is arguably an important manifestation of the idea of participatory democracy. That is, lay magistrates are the embodiment of the doctrine that true democracy requires more than periodic voting in parliamentary elections, but rather the active engagement of the citizenry in all the key spheres of decision-making (Pateman, 1970). By this means, so the argument goes, citizens become active agents in the *social contract* and the state has legitimacy because the process of governance incorporates the dynamic will of the people, something that the people at large understand and appreciate (see Richardson, 1983). According to this view, the contribution of lay magistrates goes beyond 'public spiritedness' (Raine, 1989).

Their involvement is said to be particularly important with respect to the law and the activities of lawyers because, it is suggested, lawyers mystify their trade and, like all professions, act, as G.B. Shaw put it, as a 'conspiracy against the laity'. Lay involvement in judicial decision-making ensures that the courts and those personnel and agencies who contribute to the work of the courts, are sensitised to community concerns. Some writers have interpreted the claims of participatory democracy to mean that everyone has an equal right to regular participation in decisions of general concern (see Doran and Glenn, 2000, paragraph 2.02), a proposition self-evidently more viable in relation to the jury than the lay magistracy. But participation is inevitably relative and the lay magistracy, however imperfect in terms of social representativeness,[2] must nevertheless rank high in any scale of participatory democracy.

Though none of the key documents setting out the Government's advocacy of an 'active community' specifically mentions the lay magistracy (see, for example, Active Community Unit, 1999), lay magistrates nevertheless appear to represent the sort of voluntary activity the Government says it wishes to encourage.

These participatory claims are, in practice, taken to mean that because lay magistrates are part-time and drawn from a variety of walks of life, they bring a wide experience to their decision-making. This ensures that the standards, sense of fairness and interpretation of justice applied in the magistrates' courts accords with that of the woman and man on the 'Clapham Omnibus'. Lay magistrates' justice represents a version of trial by one's peers. Lay magistrates may be socially unrepresentative, but they are closer to the ideal of trial by one's peers than can be achieved by professional judges whose background, socio-economic circumstances and lifestyle is more radically different from the defendants and witnesses typically appearing before them and whose attitudes and standards may, because of their relative social elitism, become out of kilter with those of the community at large.

The counter-view is that justice is neither simple nor a matter of common sense. It involves the dispassionate application of the rule of law; a complex set of rules designed to achieve fairness. Particularly following passage of the Human Rights Act 1998, it is sometimes said lay magistrates, even though advised by legally qualified clerks, are relatively poorly equipped to interpret and apply such complex rules.

Lawyers, by virtue of their training, are imbued with the spirit of the law and its impartial and practical application. It is argued that judges, the legal professions and the criminal justice agencies working in the courts are well aware, without the involvement of lay persons in decision-making, of public concerns regarding crime and sentencing policy. They are exposed to the same mass media as everyone else. They are recruited more broadly than the old stories of social exclusivity maintain. They daily come into contact with victims and defendants.

There is also a critical counter-view regarding magistrates' willingness to challenge prevailing court and judicial cultures to which, arguably, they are generally pleased to be co-opted and to which they tend to be deferential. Further, to the extent that lay magistrates are less effective than their legally qualified colleagues, over-reliance on lay participation runs the risk of promoting non-decision-making and delay, which may subvert due process and fairness, thereby undermining public confidence in the criminal justice system generally.

1.4.2 Local Justice vs. National Consistency

In England and Wales, lay magistrates must fulfil a local residence criterion and, despite the closure of many courthouses and the horizontal integration of PSAs and MCCs of recent years, this is a contributory element in what is referred to as *local justice*.

---

[2] Successive surveys and discussions of the membership have emphasised this point – see Royal Commission, 1948; Hood, 1972; Baldwin, 1975; Burney, 1979; King and May, 1985; Home Affairs Committee, 1996; Dignan and Whynne, 1997.

This argument is an extension of the 'Clapham Omnibus' and 'trial-by-one's-peers' viewpoint. *Local justice* includes justices knowing about local services and circumstances and being sensitive to local concerns – such factors as the prevalence of offences locally, the seriousness of offences in relation to the local economy, the typical means of defendants in relation to the local employment market and the infrastructure of services for dealing with offenders locally (Bankowski et al., 1987, 20). It is suggested that stipendiary magistrates, by contrast, are more likely to be members of a mobile career-driven cosmopolitan elite lacking local ties, knowledge and understanding.

Of course, to the extent that the latter is true, it may be accounted a benefit. If stipendiary magistrates are cosmopolitan professionals with fewer parochial ties, they may be better attuned to national decision-making standards and thus more likely to deliver greater consistency in sentencing and other decisions (a tendency arguably further advanced by the national integration of stipendiaries as district judges). It has been argued that lay magistrates, trained very largely by their justices' clerk and learning the job through a process of apprenticeship, tend to be inducted into a local *judicial culture* generative of disparity in decision-making between courts (Hood, 1972). These differences are well established and in recent years have been charted systematically (see, for example, bail and remands in custody, Jones, 1985 and Huckelsby, 1997; committal rates, Riley and Vennard, 1988 and Hedderman and Moxon, 1992; the use of different formulae for imposing fines and the size of fines, Charman et al., 1996; and sentencing generally, Tarling, 1979; Henham, 1990 and Flood-Page and Mackie, 1998). Moreover, it is said that 'local knowledge' may be an impediment to the dispensation of justice to the extent that lay magistrates are inclined to rely on what they *know*, or *believe*, to be the case as opposed to the evidence presented in court.

The suggested dichotomy between the lay and legally qualified magistrate, the part-time volunteer and the full-time specialist, the locally tied and the cosmopolitan mobile, may be to caricature the two groups. Lay magistrates are drawn overwhelmingly from the professional middle classes (see Chapter Two) and, like that sector of the population generally, are more and more geographically mobile. Stipendiaries typically occupy their posts for many years during which they develop thorough-going local knowledge.

In practice, the social composition of the lay and stipendiary magistracy is unlikely to be very different, both branches belonging to a civic social elite relatively distant from the spheres inhabited by most of the defendants appearing before them. The qualities considered desirable for recruitment to the lay magistracy and the increasingly onerous nature of a voluntary office that remains unpaid (though modest loss of earnings and expenses can be claimed) means that, ironically, there has arguably been 'indirect reinforcement of the more exclusive notion of a limited right of participation, notwithstanding official recognition of the democratic ideal of... truly representative participation' (Doran and Glenn, 2000, paragraph 2.03).

1.4.3 Fresh or Open Minds vs. Case-hardened Minds

Because lay magistrates pursue other careers, are drawn from a variety of backgrounds and do not sit every day, it is sometimes suggested that they are less likely than their stipendiary colleagues to become sceptical regarding accounts regularly proffered by defendants and to develop attitudinal affiliations with the personnel – the police, the CPS, and so on – with whom they have regular dealings. That is, they are more likely to retain open minds, to approach each case afresh, not to become 'case-hardened', less likely to learn to attach little weight to evidence from sources on which they have learned not to place reliance. By contrast, the stipendiaries are said to accumulate prejudices as to who is credible.

The counter argument is that stipendiaries, by virtue of their legal training and the personal confidence which they acquire by virtue of their legal training, are able more effectively to challenge the accounts they receive from defendants and regular court users alike.

According to this viewpoint, lay magistrates, like jurors, may be either overly deferential (to the prosecution) or gullible or naïve (regarding defence accounts). To the extent that the latter is true, it results in an irony: the evidence most used in support of the proposition that some decisions result from case-hardening – the substantially higher acquittal rate in the Crown Court compared to magistrates' courts (Home Office, 2000a, Chapter Six) – is used *against* magistrates, which largely means lay magistrates, *in favour* of juries.

If there is a continuum for case-hardening, most observers would probably place lay magistrates far closer to the end of the continuum occupied by professional judges than that occupied by jurors. There is some research evidence, for example, that magistrates are more likely than juries to convict on the basis of prosecution accounts of events (especially evidence from police witnesses) in cases where defendants deny the alleged conduct and/or the requisite criminal intent (see Vennard, 1981; Vennard, 1985).

1.4.4 Symbolic Legitimacy vs. Effectiveness and Efficiency

It has been argued, as we have seen, that lay participation in judicial decision-making serves to legitimise the criminal justice process. Whether that is in fact the case is an issue that we shall explore (see Chapter Five). In the meantime we shall describe this argument as one of symbolic legitimacy. Even if the evidence supports the contention, it may be counterpoised by the argument that in order to preserve their lay qualities – an essential element in lay magistrates' claim to confer democratic legitimacy – the working arrangements for lay magistrates must make their participation both relatively ineffective and inefficient, about which the public at large may be little aware. For example, the Lord Chancellor lays down guidelines restricting the sittings of lay magistrates and, because the organisation of lay magistrates is largely non-hierarchical, the number of sittings each does is ideally more or less equal. Intermittent sittings arranged randomly so that the composition of tribunals rotates, makes it relatively difficult for the lay magistracy to provide continuity in case handling. A high proportion of cases is not dealt with during a single appearance (see Mahoney, 2000). It follows that, generally speaking, successive appearances are before different panels of lay magistrates unfamiliar with preceding events and about which they must be enlightened.

Further, because it is unlikely that part-time lay magistrates will have the confidence of full-time lawyer magistrates, it is asserted that lay magistrates are fair game for advocates wishing to engage in time-wasting and other costly tactics deployed for their own or their clients' advantage. Stipendiaries, it is supposed, are better equipped to resist such ploys (NAO, 1999, paragraph 4.62).

1.4.5 Cost

It has traditionally been assumed that because lay magistrates are unpaid volunteers, they are necessarily cheaper than their stipendiary colleagues. However, it is not clear that this is the case (Home Office, 1997a, 25). Were the indirect costs taken into account – the provision of legally-qualified clerks to advise them, the administrative support necessary for their recruitment, training and rota arrangements, the provision of additional courtrooms required by what the available limited evidence suggests is their slower decision-making (Seago, Walker and Wall, 1995), the knock-on costs incurred by other criminal justice agencies resulting from their possible relative inefficiency, and so on – it is far from clear that reliance on lay magistrates leads to cost savings. This is a question that we have specifically been asked to address.

Some of the arguments set out above are based on stereotypes. Others comprise a mixture of evidence and prejudice. Others still are ideological. Taken together they also generate potential inconsistencies or competing short- and long-term considerations. For example, the Government attaches considerable importance to both volunteering and the creation of an active community (and the existence of lay magistrates must be taken to figure prominently in the realisation of that ideal), and to effectiveness, efficiency and economy in the delivery of public services (the engine behind many of the changes in the reorganisation of the Magistrates' Courts Service which both lay and stipendiary magistrates least like). Competing interpretations of independence and accountability, local and national, are at stake here (see Seago, Walker and Wall, 2000). We shall not attempt to resolve these potential contradictions. In the report that follows we shall assess the validity of as many of the competing arguments described above as we are able so that those whose task it is to make policy can do so on the basis of good evidence.

1.5   THE NATURE AND TIMING OF THE RESEARCH

The research was commissioned in late autumn 1999 and was focused on ten PSAs representing different types of court business, with and without full-time stipendiaries.

The chief executive for the MCC of each PSA was first contacted, followed by the justices' clerk. The nature of the research was explained and outline agreement for participation sought. Meetings were then arranged which, typically, the chairman of the bench also attended. The basis for selection was confirmed. This included the criterion of relative administrative stability. Though, for reasons discussed above, there is scarcely a court in England and Wales that *has not* been affected in the last year or two by amalgamation or other major administrative changes, we wished to avoid courts subject to immediate disruption, particularly during the planned fieldwork period. We did not want, for example, to include courts to which stipendiaries had only recently been appointed, which were the subject of pilots for new legislation or administrative innovation and which were already the subject of research.

In the event, the early advice we received from the LCD proved well-founded and all ten of the selected courts were judged suitable and agreed to take part. Because of the concerns which many lay magistrates have about current developments and their future role, bench meetings were arranged during February and March 2000. At these meetings the research rationale and plan was fully explained and questions answered. It was generally felt that these bench meetings were invaluable in gaining acceptance of, and co-operation with, the data-collection process. The principal characteristics of the ten courts are set out in Figure 1.2.

Figure 1.2

Court sample characteristics

Court	MCC Area Description	Total Proceeded Against in 1998	Number of Lay Magistrates	Stipendiary Magistrates
Rural 1	Shire	<5000	55	None
Rural 2	Shire	5,000 – 10,000	88	None
Mixed Urban Rural	Shire	5,000 – 10,000	85	2 part-time
Urban 1	Shire	5,000 – 10,000	124	None
Urban 2	Shire	5,000 – 10,000	129	None
Urban 3	Metropolitan	> 20,000	470	2 full-time
Provincial Metropolitan 1	Metropolitan	> 20,000	353	3 full-time
Provincial Metropolitan 2	Metropolitan	> 20,000	328	3 full-time
Outer London	London	5,000 – 10,000	138	1 full-time
Inner London	London	< 5,000	58	5 full-time

In relation to each of the ten courts, the following categories of data were collected (for further information see Appendix B):

- baseline information regarding court budgets, buildings, court staff, magistrates' characteristics and sittings, and so on
- self-completed magistrates' diary data, for stipendiary and lay magistrates, for a period of six weeks, 27 March – 6 May 2000
- self-completed magistrates' questionnaires, for stipendiary and lay magistrates, regarding current sitting arrangements and views regarding altering the balance between lay and stipendiary magistrates
- observations of court appearances during April – May 2000
- telephone interviews in May 2000 with a sample of court users regarding their perceptions of lay and stipendiary magistrates' performance.

It was planned that court register data, providing basic information about all court appearances, would for the period of the court observations be transferred electronically to the research team and analysed separately to provide a much larger data set on which to map the more detailed material gathered from the sample of observed court appearances. In the event this exercise proved not to be feasible technically, except in one or two courts.

In addition to this local fieldwork, meetings were held with various persons in the LCD and with the Chief Metropolitan Stipendiary Magistrate and his staff. Data were provided from these sources about lay and stipendiary magistrates generally. Data were also provided by the Home Office regarding magistrates' courts' workloads nationally. The information collected from these national sources enabled us to map the court observation data onto the universe of magistrates' courts and court appearances and thus estimate the national implications of the patterns established locally.

Two other data collection exercises were undertaken. In June 2000 a public opinion survey was conducted to find out the degree to which the public is aware of the composition of magistrates' court adjudicators and to elicit views about magistrates' performance. Finally, in order to gather information about the involvement of lay persons in judicial decision-making in other jurisdictions, contact was made with knowledgeable persons in other countries. As part of this exercise, the Directorate of Legal Affairs within the Council of Europe, Strasbourg, kindly agreed to send our brief questionnaire to the governments of all 41 Council of Europe member states seeking information.

This report is based, therefore, on a complicated data collection exercise conducted largely between February and June 2000, preceded by two months of planning and followed by two and a half months of data analysis and writing up. A more detailed account of the data collection methods we adopted is contained in Appendix B.

1.6   THE STRUCTURE OF THE REPORT

The plan of the report is based largely on the different categories of data as follows.

Chapter Two concerns what lay and stipendiary magistrates do – their sitting patterns, the nature of the business undertaken by them and the degree to which they work together. It is based largely on magistrates' self-completed diaries, though with some reference to their self-completed questionnaires and information gathered locally from court administrative staff and nationally from the LCD and the office of the Chief Metropolitan Stipendiary Magistrate. Chapter Three concerns how lay and stipendiary magistrates do what they do. It is based almost entirely on the court observational data. Chapter Four reports the opinions of regular court users, based on interviews with them, regarding the performance of lay and stipendiary magistrates.

Chapter Five reports what the public at large knows about and thinks regarding the performance of magistrates. Chapter Six comprises a cost analysis of the contribution of lay and stipendiary magistrates and the likely consequences of altering the balance of the contribution that the two groups currently make. This chapter draws on a variety of data, principally baseline budgetary information and the court observational and national magistrates' courts workload data sets. Chapter Seven comprises a brief survey of the degree to which lay persons are involved in judicial decision-making in other jurisdictions and the different models for their participation. Chapter Eight draws together what the study has revealed and the possible implications of the findings for future policy.

2 WHO ARE THE MAGISTRATES AND WHAT DO THEY DO?

When we embarked on the fieldwork for this study there were approximately 30,400 lay magistrates, 96 full-time and 146 part-time stipendiary magistrates in England and Wales. In this chapter we shall consider the membership of the two groups and the contribution they make to the working of the magistrates' courts.

2.1 THE LAY MAGISTRACY: THE DEMANDS OF THE OFFICE

Potential lay magistrates are advised that they must be willing to undertake a minimum of 26 half-day court sittings per annum and normally be prepared and able to sit rather more frequently – generally between 35 and 45 sittings per annum. The Lord Chancellor has advised lay magistrates that it is not appropriate that they undertake more than 70 sittings in the adult court and 100 sittings per annum across all the specialist panels (or in Inner London, the entirely separate adult and youth courts) of which they may be members.

Though sitting in court is the activity for which lay magistrates are appointed, it is by no means their only activity. They receive training both initially and continuously to perform specialist functions and keep up-to-date. They mentor and appraise each other. If they wish to chair panels they must be willing to train for the task. They are encouraged to play a part in the life and administration of the court – attend bench meetings, sit on liaison and administrative committees and represent the bench on local fora. Many benches take a pride in the fact that their members undertake various activities to educate the community at large about the role of the magistracy and the work of magistrates' courts. Finally, there are some duties which are performed outside the court setting: hearing applications from the police for search warrants; witnessing statutory declarations; visiting licensed premises preparatory to hearing licence renewals; reading case papers in advance of hearings, and so on. Once a person has been appointed a lay magistrate, he or she exercises a wide discretion as to how many of these activities to get involved in and to what degree.

There is, then, a wide margin of appreciation as to what is involved in being a lay magistrate. How this margin is interpreted, both individually and collectively, partly determines who is thought suitable for appointment and who is able and willing to take on what is a relatively onerous but unpaid voluntary office. These considerations naturally affect the degree to which the lay magistracy is, and is ever likely to be, representative of the community at large. Given that it has been a longstanding observation and complaint that the lay magistracy in England and Wales is not representative of the community at large (see Chapter One), what is the current situation and exactly how much time do existing lay magistrates devote to the office?

2.2 LAY MAGISTRATES AND THE COMMUNITY: REPRESENTATIVENESS

We address the issue of lay magistrates' representativeness in relation to gender, age, ethnicity and employment status. In addition to information gathered from the records of the clerks for the ten participating courts, we have also drawn on the answers given by respondents to our survey of magistrates and data held centrally by the LCD. We shall not consider magistrates' party political affiliations or preferences: data were supplied to us on this question but they were too out-of-date (they related to preferences at the time of appointment) to be meaningful, not least because they were not capable of being compared to public preferences locally at the time of the most recent general election.

2.2.1 Gender

The lay magistracy is, and for some time now has been, gender balanced. Forty-nine per cent of lay magistrates nationally are women. Across the ten participating courts almost exactly half of the magistrates are women, though the figures for individual courts range from 41 to 53 per cent. This gender balance stands in marked contrast to the overwhelmingly male ranks of the judges and stipendiary magistrates.

2.2.2 Age

According to LCD records, very few magistrates are appointed in their 20s and remarkably few magistrates nationally (4%) are under 40 years of age. By contrast almost a third (32%) are in their 60s (they must retire on reaching the age of 70). The ten participating benches broadly reflect this national pattern, though they include marginally more younger and older magistrates. However, there is a good deal of variation between benches. One semi-rural bench, for example, has not a single member under 40 years of age and 43 per cent of its members are 60 or over. By contrast 10 per cent of both the London benches are in their 30s and one of the rural benches has only 19 per cent of its members aged 60 or more (see Figure A.1, Appendix A).

2.2.3 Ethnicity

It has been a longstanding complaint that the lay magistracy is overwhelmingly white and fails to represent the increasing ethnic diversity of contemporary Britain. This criticism is less applicable today than it has ever been.

Ninety-four per cent of the population in England and Wales is white, two per cent is black, three per cent is of Indian sub-continent or Asian origin and a further one per cent is drawn from other groups. The precise complexion of the lay magistracy is not known because the ethnic identity of 11 per cent of its membership is recorded as unknown. However, if this 11 per cent is assumed to be white – and every informed person we have consulted has suggested that this is a reasonable assumption – then the composition of the lay magistracy nationally is now approaching ethnic representativeness, that is, two per cent black, two per cent of Indian sub-continent or Asian origin and one per cent other (see Figure A.2, Appendix A).

This is the picture nationally: there are substantial variations locally and, more importantly, the fit between local benches and the make-up of the local communities they serve is, in several instances, wide. Two aspects of the data in Figure 2.1 are worthy of note. First, if it is possible for two of the participating benches (one smallish and one very large) to be able to record the ethnicity of all members, it is hard to understand why two other benches (one small and one very large) record 15 per cent as of unknown ethnicity: one can only assume that the question is not regarded by those courts as particularly important.

Secondly, with one exception (a smallish semi-rural bench of which not a single member is non-white, though two to three per cent of the local population is), those benches serving areas with ethnic minority composition at or below the national average level, have achieved above average representation of the ethnic minorities in their own ranks, and vice versa. Which is to say that it is in those areas with very large ethnic minorities – the London area and one of our provincial urban courts – that the lay magistracy, despite having recruited many non-white members, remains disproportionately white.

Figure 2.1

Ethnic breakdown of sample benches

Area by Postcode	White		Black Caribbean, Black African, Black other		Indian, Pakistani, Bangladeshi, Chinese, other Asian		Other		Not known		Total
	Local pop.	Bench	Local pop.	Bench	Local pop.	Bench	Local pop.	Bench	Local pop.	Bench	
Rural 1	99%	96%	0%	0%	1%	0%	0%	0%	-	4%	100%
Rural 2	99%	84%	0%	0%	1%	1%	0%	0%	-	15%	100%
Mixed urban rural	97%	100%	1%	0%	1%	0%	0%	0%	-	0%	100%
Urban 1	96%	90%	1%	3%	2%	3%	1%	1%	-	2%	100%
Urban 2	88%	88%	3%	0%	9%	4%	1%	2%	-	6%	100%
Urban 3	89%	77%	5%	2%	5%	3%	1%	1%	-	17%	100%
Provincial Metropolitan 1	98%	94%	1%	2%	1%	4%	0%	0%	-	0%	100%
Provincial Metropolitan 2	94%	90%	2%	5%	3%	3%	1%	0%	-	2%	100%
Inner & outer London #	66%	76%	13%	6%	19%	9%	2%	2%	-	7%	100%

Source: Justices' clerks' records and 1991 Census

Due to considerable variations within London data, these areas are combined to provide a figure for London as a whole

2.2.4 Occupation and Social Status

The LCD currently employs a classification of lay magistrates' occupational status different from all others in common use. Comparison with, for example, national census data is therefore not possible (though the LCD is developing a database using the census classification). The LCD categories 'employees of national companies' and 'employees of local companies/organisations' fail to distinguish salaried managing directors from part-time hourly-paid unskilled workers. The category 'farmers and other agricultural workers' does not distinguish wealthy landowners from lowly-paid farm labourers. 'Local government employees' are not sub-classified by status. 'Not in paid employment/retired' does not distinguish persons seeking employment from those who are not.

Further, the LCD data are collected when magistrates are appointed and are likely, therefore, to be out-of-date. It follows that it is not easy to assess the validity of the commonly made criticism that the lay magistracy is overwhelmingly well-off and middle class, relatively distanced from the socio-economic circumstances of the majority of criminal defendants. Within the data recorded by justices' clerks and reported to the LCD and the responses to our questionnaires, however, are indications of the relative socio-economic circumstances of lay magistrates.

Across the eight participating benches, one-quarter of magistrates (26%) are described, according to LCD records, as not in paid employment/retired, a further quarter (25%) are lecturers/teachers, healthcare professionals (e.g. doctors/nurses) or other professionals (e.g. accountants/surveyors), [1] and 13 per cent are self-employed (see Figure A.3, Appendix A).

Respondents to our questionnaire were asked to record their usual occupation and, if retired, to record their usual occupation prior to retirement. A clearer picture of lay magistrates' occupational status emerges from this source. Most significant is the fact that two-fifths (40%) of magistrates say that they are retired (compared to the 26% on LCD files described as not in employment *or* retired). More than two-thirds (69%) give as their current or former occupation a professional or managerial position, 12 per cent say that they have clerical or other non-manual jobs, three per cent are skilled manual workers and five per cent say they are unemployed. We are unable to say what proportion are self-employed and it is of course possible that a proportion of both those who say they have retired and those who say that they are employed, work part-time.

If the proportion of the magistracy drawn from professional and managerial backgrounds is compared to the profile of the populations local to their courts (see Figure 2.2), then the differences are striking. These occupations are over-represented in the ranks of the magistracy by between two and four times. In even the most representative bench, serving an affluent urban area, 63 per cent of the bench have managerial or professional occupations compared to 31 per cent of the local population. In the most extreme case, a deprived metropolitan area, 79 per cent of the bench members say that they are professionals or managers compared to only 20 per cent of the local population.

The lay magistracy is disproportionately middle class, and almost certainly financially well-off, compared to the population at large.

If the duties of lay magistrates are relatively onerous as well as being unpaid, it is not surprising that the composition of benches consists overwhelmingly of persons with the time and personal resources to bear that burden. Eighty-six per cent of the magistrates who completed our questionnaire told us that they do not claim any loss of earnings – including 76 per cent of the 60 per cent of magistrates who say they are employed – and almost one-quarter (23%) say that they seldom or never claim expenses.

These facts cannot be taken entirely to reflect magistrates' advantageous financial situation. Some working magistrates, whether self-employed or employed, [2] are no doubt able to arrange their sittings so that they do not intrude on their working hours. Others have employers who are content to allow them to take time off work without any deduction being made from their salaries. [3]

---

[1] These figures are calculated from the magistrates' self-classification.
[2] Part-time employees may also arrange all their sittings in their own time and consider this as a leisure activity.
[3] Section 59 of the 1975 Employment Protection Act states that an employer should permit an employee who is a justice of the peace to take time off their employment, although it does not state this should be paid.

Figure 2.2

Professional/Managerial make-up of sample benches and local population[1]

		Percentage within the occupation category Professional/Managerial
Rural 1	Bench	63%
	Local population	22%
Rural 2	Bench	66%
	Local population	22%
Mixed Urban-rural	Bench	73%
	Local population	23%
Urban 1	Bench	63%
	Local population	31%
Urban 2	Bench	60%
	Local population	23%
Urban 3	Bench	68%
	Local population	22%
Prov Met 1	Bench	79%
	Local population	20%
Prov Met 2	Bench	66%
	Local population	24%
Outer London	Bench	72%
	Local population	21%
Inner London	Bench	66%
	Local population	21%

Source of bench figures: Magistrates' questionnaire: lay magistrate self-classification

[1] Source of local population in the 1991 Census

In our judgement there would be merit in the LCD knowing more about these issues. In addition to gathering data regarding the *current* occupational status of the lay magistracy and using the same classification as is used in the census, there would be a case for occasionally surveying lay magistrates to discover on what basis, and at what cost, they are able to fulfil the increasingly onerous demands of the office. If the lay magistracy is to be made more socially representative of the population at large, these are important issues.

2.3   LAY MAGISTRATES' SITTINGS: ACTUAL AND IDEAL

Two measures were collected of lay magistrates' sittings. Firstly, the records supplied by the clerks for each of the participating courts. Secondly, the answers to the questionnaires completed by 1,120 of the 1,830[4] magistrates (61%) making up the ten participating benches: respondents were asked to estimate their annual number of sittings. The two measures are not straightforwardly comparable. The former is an objective record of the sittings achieved during the most recent period of 12 months for all magistrates. The latter comprises estimates for a generalised year and, as such, perhaps represents more the aspirations of the sample of magistrates who responded (though the respondents were broadly representative of the ten benches – see Appendix B for notes on the survey methodology).

The average actual number of sittings for lay magistrates across all ten courts, as reported by the clerks, is 41.4 (see Figure 2.3). The average for individual courts ranges from 32.5 to 46.2. The smaller, more rural courts record the lowest average sittings. But the pattern is uneven. The largest urban court in the sample (39.3) lies close to the overall average number of sittings, as does one of the two London courts (38.1).

More striking are the differences in the number of sittings between individual magistrates. Whereas 15 per cent manage fewer than the minimum 26 sittings required (though this figure includes some newly-appointed magistrates in post for less than a year, as well as those who, because of long-term sickness or the weight of other commitments, were unable to make their required quota), 11 per cent sit 66 times a year or more. Twenty magistrates out of 1,828 (1%) sat more than 100 times. These data are the basis for our classification, used in Chapter Three, of bench chairmen as 'infrequent' (35 or fewer sittings per annum), 'average' (36 to 45 sittings) and 'frequent' (46 sittings or more) sitters.

The results from the questionnaire show that magistrates think that they sit rather more frequently than in fact they do: they say that they sit on average 49 times a year compared to the 41.4 achieved. Only five per cent report sitting less than 26 times a year whereas 16 per cent say that they sit more than 65 times. Moreover, when asked how often they would ideally like to sit their average response is 54, a figure 30 per cent higher than the actuality and more than twice as high as the minimum asked of them. The higher rate results from most magistrates with average or low actual sittings saying that they are willing to sit more often (only 14% say that they would like to sit less than 40 times a year compared to the 26% who say that they do sit that often). The proportion of magistrates wishing to sit more often than 65 times a year is only marginally higher than the proportion who say that they already do (20% compared to 16%). Older magistrates are more willing to undertake high numbers of sittings.

Magistrates' ideal number of sittings is conditioned by what duties are currently undertaken by them. Magistrates in rural courts sit less often than magistrates in the large urban courts (in both London and the provinces) and they wish to sit less often. The reverse is the case for benches with high sitting rates. Older, long-service magistrates already sit more often than younger short-service colleagues and are the most willing to sit even more often (see Figure A.4, Appendix A).

---

[4] Due to small differences in the reporting periods the clerks' data contained information on 1,828 magistrates. This was two fewer than the number invited to take part in the survey research.

Figure 2.3

Magistrates' sittings per annum in the sample courts

Sittings	Data	Rural 1	Rural 2	Mixed urban – rural	Urban 1	Urban 2	Urban 3	Metrop olitan 1	Metrop olitan 2	Outer London	Inner London	Total
0–25	Number	8	13	20	16	15	81	35	54	33	9	284
	%	15%	15%	24%	13%	12%	17%	10%	16%	24%	16%	15%
26–35	Number	14	11	25	25	32	106	72	71	43	15	414
	%	25%	13%	29%	20%	25%	23%	20%	22%	31%	26%	23%
36–45	Number	21	29	25	28	32	120	101	87	28	14	485
	%	38%	33%	29%	23%	25%	26%	29%	27%	20%	24%	27%
46–55	Number	9	25	13	27	21	78	56	52	10	5	296
	%	16%	28%	15%	22%	16%	17%	16%	16%	7%	9%	16%
56–65	Number	1	9	2	13	11	48	27	26	4	2	143
	%	2%	10%	2%	10%	9%	10%	8%	8%	3%	3%	8%
> 65	Number	2	1		15	18	37	62	38	20	13	206
	%	4%	1%	0%	12%	14%	8%	18%	12%	14%	22%	11%
Total Number		55	88	85	124	129	470	353	328	138	58	1,828
Total %		100%	100%	100%	100%	100%	100%	100%	100%	100%	100%	100%
Total Average		36.1	39.0	32.5	44.3	43.9	39.3	46.2	41.5	45.7	38.1	41.4

Source: Justices' Clerks' records

The majority of magistrates (72%) say that their actual number of sittings is close to their ideal. Those magistrates who sit relatively infrequently are least likely to say that their number of sittings is what they would like to be the case (59% for those sitting less than 30 times a year).

The 27 per cent of magistrates who say that their ideal and actual number of sittings is not close give rather different reasons for the fact depending on whether they are currently infrequent or frequent sitters (Figure 2.4). Magistrates who sit relatively infrequently tend to say that they "would like to take on more sittings, but I cannot spare the time at present" (60% of those with under 45 sittings, 19% with 45 or more sittings). The minority of frequent sitters, who say that their current rate of sitting is not ideal for them, are split between those wanting to undertake more sittings (or having greater responsibility when they sit) and those wanting to undertake fewer sittings, or feeling that they have to take the chair or sit on specialist panels because of a shortage of people "like them".

Figure 2.4

Frequently sitting magistrates' reasons for differences between their ideal and current number of sittings

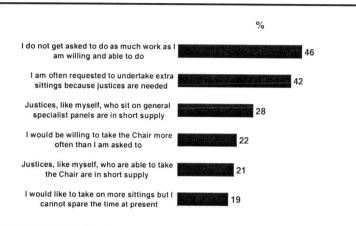

Base: All lay magistrates who are frequent sitters (112)

Source: Lay magistrates' questionnaire

2.4   THE DISTRIBUTION OF SITTINGS WITHIN BENCHES

All magistrates, lay and stipendiary, were asked whether lay magistrates should undertake an approximately equal number of sittings within each bench. Whereas a bare majority of the stipendiaries (56%) think that sittings should be equal in number, fewer than a third (30%) of lay magistrates agree, with the largest group (47%) having no strong feelings on the issue (Figure 2.5). Magistrates from smaller rural benches (where average sittings are lowest), younger magistrates, and infrequent sitters are most likely to favour equality of sittings.

Figure 2.5

Magistrates' views on whether lay justices should undertake an approximately equal number of sittings within each bench

	Stipen-diary	Lay magistrates						
	Total	Total	Court area type			Age		
			Lon-don	Urb-an	Rural	Under 44	45–64	65+
Base: All respondents	27	1,120	126	832	162	123	814	173
	%	%	%	%	%	%	%	%
Yes	56	30	32	27	48	36	29	29
No	7	22	21	24	11	21	22	20
No strong feelings	37	47	43	49	41	41	48	50
Not stated	-	1	4	*	4	1	1	1

Source: Magistrates' questionnaire

The perceived benefits of an equal number of sittings are similar for all magistrate sub-groups. Respondents say, unprompted, that equal numbers of sittings means, in order of importance, that:

- all colleagues gain similar or the same experience
- the work is shared
- decision-making is balanced
- the overall level of competence is maintained.

Lay magistrates, however, are more aware than their stipendiary colleagues of the drawbacks of equal numbers of sittings. They say – and the pattern of responses is similar for all sub-groups – that:

- people have different amounts of time to give or different outside commitments (56%)
- there is need for flexibility, or that an emphasis on equality of sitting would mean losing flexibility (11%)
- there are increasing demands or more pressure being put on magistrates (6%)
- any demand that there be equal sittings would be difficult for court administrators to organise (5%).

If the number of sittings is not to be shared equally between magistrates then the question of whether a ceiling should be placed on the number of sittings any individual magistrate undertakes, as the Lord Chancellor considers appropriate, comes to the fore. About three-quarters of magistrates, lay and stipendiary, agree that there should be an upper limit both as regards sittings in the adult court and in all panels combined. There is less agreement about what the upper limit should be. Stipendiary magistrates call for a lower limit than lay magistrates and, among lay magistrates, older magistrates and those from rural benches call for lower maxima than their urban and younger colleagues. Frequent sitters, not surprisingly, defend a higher limit than do infrequent sitters (Figures A.5 and A.6, Appendix A).

2.5   LAY MAGISTRATES: TOTAL TIME COMMITMENT

All 1,830 lay members of the ten participating benches were asked to keep a diary for the six week period 27 March to 6 May 2000. They were asked to record all the time devoted to their office of magistrate and, if in doubt as to whether an activity is magistrate-related, to include it. Details of the methodology for this part of the study are set out in Appendix B. The six week diary was completed in two parts of three weeks each: 1,151 magistrates completed the first part and 868 the second. The following analysis is therefore based on 2,019 three-week magistrate activity diaries.

Lay magistrates in the sample recorded an average of 0.9 court sittings per week, or 46.8 per year (Figure 2.6). This is somewhat higher than the average number of sittings (41.4) known to have been completed in the most recent period of 12 months. These figures may be higher because they exclude the summer period when most annual leave is likely to be taken.

The magistrates reported the average court sitting lasting approximately two and a half hours (156 minutes), but involving a further 52 minutes in the courthouse but outside the court. Lay magistrates are asked to arrive well before the court sits so as to learn of their court allocation, sign the register, pick up court lists and other accompanying papers as necessary and be advised by their legal advisor about any unusual matters coming before them. Further, after the court rises they may have to fill in appraisal forms, or consult the clerk or colleagues about bench-related matters. The average lay magistrate therefore spends on average 188 minutes per week in the courthouse. The average for rural areas is lower than that for urban areas and London and lower for younger than for older magistrates, no doubt a reflection of the greater responsibilities (including chairmanship) carried by more experienced colleagues. To the time spent in the courthouse must be added the travelling time taken to get there and back, 44 minutes on average, 25 minutes in rural areas, 45 minutes in urban areas and 61 minutes in London.

More than half (57%) of the three-week diaries recorded no activity other than court sittings. Twelve per cent recorded three or more other activities, however. Training and bench administrative and liaison meetings figured most prominently, though a significant number of magistrates recorded what can best be described as community relations activities. Though it is probable that commitments such as membership of key bench committees is concentrated in relatively few and experienced hands, it is likely that the overwhelming majority of magistrates take part, at some stage in the year, in training and bench meetings. The diary survey shows that the average lay justice takes part in 0.36 activities other than court sittings per week and, if travelling time is included, devotes an additional 48 minutes to these activities (Figure 2.7). This equates to more than a full working week each year – 41.6 hours – though most training sessions take place during the evenings and on Saturdays, outside normal working hours.

Figure 2.6

Lay magistrates: time spent in court (per week)

	Court area type			Age			Total
	London	Urban	Rural	Under 45	45–64	65+	
Average number of court sittings	0.97	0.93	0.65	0.67	0.89	1.04	0.90
Average time per court sitting (mins)	150	154	180	152	156	155	156
Average time in courthouse per sitting other than sitting in court (mins)	61	51	41	49	53	49	52
Average time per week sat in court (mins)	145	143	117	102	140	160	141
Average time per week in courthouse other than sitting in court (mins)	59	47	27	33	47	51	47
Total time spent in courthouse (mins)	204	190	144	135	187	211	188
Total time spent travelling	61	45	25	33	43	54	44

Because the diaries covered only a short period they may have been unduly affected by chance factors, such as whether a particular bench happened to have a major meeting during the recording period. It follows that too much reliance cannot be placed on apparent differences between the ten benches. Nevertheless members of the London and smaller rural benches recorded many more activities than did their colleagues in the provincial urban and metropolitan courts, and this pattern was consistent with what the clerks to justices had earlier told us to expect about their magistrates' participation in corporate bench activities. The evidence suggests that there are significant differences between the cultures of benches in this respect. Some benches are almost certainly more active than others.

Figure 2.7

Lay magistrates' time spent engaged in non-court activities (per week)

	Court area type			Age			Total
	London	Urban	Rural	Under 45	45–64	65+	
Average number of other activities	0.53	0.29	0.60	0.23	0.37	0.40	0.36
Average time per activity (mins)	137	119	118	112	123	120	122
Average travel time involved in other activities (mins)	14	12	9	10	12	11	12
Average time per week in other activities (mins)	72	35	71	26	45	48	44
Average travel time per week in other activities (mins)	8	3	6	2	4	4	4
Total time spent in other activities (mins)	80	38	77	28	49	52	48

It is not clear, however, how important these differences are for the effectiveness of the lay magistracy and for their credibility with the public at large. How vital, for example, is it that some lay magistrates in some areas devote themselves to educating community groups about the work of the magistrates' courts? Do such activities aid the recruitment of minority community group members to the magistracy? Do they enhance the legitimacy with the public at large of the criminal courts? We do not have answers to these questions, but they are important when it comes to consideration of an alteration in the balance of the contribution made by lay and stipendiary magistrates. Were there to be more stipendiary magistrates, what exactly should they be employed to do?

2.6 STIPENDIARY MAGISTRATES: NUMBERS AND TERMS OF APPOINTMENT

Stipendiary magistrates are full- or part-time appointees, appointed hitherto to a particular commission area on the basis of a request from the Lord Chancellor's Advisory Committee that a stipendiary be appointed, and the Lord Chancellor agreeing it is appropriate. There are ceilings as to how many full-time stipendiary magistrates there may be in London and the provinces which, over time, have progressively been raised. There are currently 47 stipendiaries in London and 49 in the provinces; 96 in all (for a more detailed account of the history and appointment of stipendiary magistrates, see Seago, Walker and Wall, 1995). There are (or were in spring 2000) also 146 part-time or acting stipendiary magistrates nationally, subject to four-year appointments.

The fact that stipendiaries have, until now, been appointed to particular commission areas has meant that any stipendiary asked to assist a court in a commission area other than that to which he or she is appointed has had to be issued with a letter of temporary appointment. This cumbersome arrangement is being changed: district judges, as stipendiaries are now to be called, are to be appointed normally to sit in a particular locality, but will be capable of temporarily sitting, by agreement and without need for a letter of appointment, wherever else they are needed.

Stipendiaries' letters of appointment stipulate that they will undertake judicial duties five days a week. This translates, when annual and Bank Holidays are taken into account, to 44 weeks or 220 days per annum. Judicial duties include court sittings within and without stipendiaries' appointed commission areas and the performance of other judicial offices to which individual stipendiaries may have been appointed (27 of the 96 stipendiaries, or 28%, are dual post-holders – mostly recorders or assistant recorders, though a few in London are immigration adjudicators or tribunal members). Judicial duties also include approved judicial activities such as attendance at Judicial Studies Board training events and periodic national meetings of stipendiaries, assisting with the recruitment or training of new stipendiaries, and so on.

It is unclear, however, what a full-time stipendiary appointment does or should mean in terms of the number of court sittings undertaken each year. The uncertainty results from two factors. First, there has been an understanding historically that stipendiaries in London will not routinely sit in court on as many weekdays as their colleagues in the provinces. London stipendiaries have been expected, on a rota basis, to undertake certain duties – being on call to hear applications for extended police detention of suspects under the Police and Criminal Evidence Act 1984, sitting on Saturdays or Bank Holidays, a few of them undertaking extradition hearings on a rota basis and other colleagues, on the family court, hearing emergency protection order applications, also on a rota basis – not normally expected of stipendiaries in the provinces. Secondly, the fact that there is no guidance about the number of court sittings (as there is for lay magistrates) means that the amount of time it is reasonable for stipendiaries *not* to be sitting in court during five weekdays is to some extent negotiable, particularly when scheduled court lists collapse.

As in the case of lay magistrates, we have collected two measures of stipendiaries' court sittings. First, because there is no single collated record of all their court sittings, we have attempted to compile an account for the 16 stipendiaries appointed to six of the ten courts participating in the study on the basis of records kept by justices' clerks locally and the office of the Chief Metropolitan Magistrate in London and, with respect to approved temporary sittings outside commission areas, the LCD centrally. Secondly, we have considered the self-completed diaries returned to us by 27 (full-time and part-time) stipendiary magistrates for 49 three-week periods between 27 March and 6 May 2000 (see Appendix B for details of the methodology). The results from applying these two methods suggest that there is some variation in how often stipendiaries actually sit in court. Because this is an issue of considerable importance when calculating the cost and other implications of altering the balance between the contribution made by lay and stipendiary magistrates, we shall address it in some detail below.

2.7   WHO ARE THE STIPENDIARIES?

Full-time stipendiaries, unlike lay magistrates, are mostly male (currently 84% of them) and though they are never young (none is currently under 45 years of age) and are overwhelmingly middle aged, they are substantially less likely to be over 60 than their lay colleagues (16% compared to 32%). Indeed, more than half (54%) are aged 45 to 54. Currently, two are drawn from the ethnic minorities (if those whose ethnicity is not recorded are accounted white – the same assumption as we have applied to lay magistrates above).

Stipendiaries must be barristers or solicitors. The solicitors predominate (64%), though the proportion of barristers among London stipendiaries is greater than in the provinces (42% compared to 27%) (Figure 2.8). A quarter (26%) have previously been clerks to justices: this career step is more common among provincial than London stipendiaries (33% compared to 19%).

Full-time stipendiaries are almost invariably appointed in their 40s (though they have all served as part-time stipendiaries previously, during their four year apprenticeship) and the growth in the number of provincial stipendiaries in recent years means that most of them have served full-time for far fewer years than their lay colleagues have served part-time. Whereas 78 per cent of stipendiaries have full-time service of ten years or less, the majority of lay magistrates (53%) have been in office for more than ten years.

Figure 2.8

Stipendiary magistrates: length of service (years) and professional background

Years in office	Total	Barrister	Barrister/ former clerk to justices	Solicitor	Solicitor/ former clerk to justices
0 – 5	26	5	4	14	3
6 – 10	49	10	5	23	11
11 – 15	14	5	–	7	2
16+	7	4	–	3	–
Total	96	24	9	47	16

2.8 STIPENDIARY COURT SITTINGS

The data collected from courts locally and the LCD centrally failed unequivocally to show how many court sittings were made during the most recent twelve month period by each of the 16 stipendiaries in the six participating courts with stipendiary appointments. Clerks to justices generally record only sittings made in their own courts as opposed to, for example, the Crown Court or those outside their commission areas. The LCD records only those temporary appointments when stipendiaries sit in commission areas other than their own. The office of the Chief Metropolitan Magistrate reckons on having a fairly complete account of sittings made by London stipendiaries, no matter where they sit.

The sittings of the ten provincial stipendiaries in the court sample appear to range between 329 and 416 per annum, though in half the cases we have been unable to resolve differences in the records kept locally and centrally. If the midpoint is taken in those cases where we have been unable to resolve differences, and if the sittings of one stipendiary are discounted on the grounds that he was in post for less than a full year, then 368 is the average number of sittings achieved. This suggests that on 72 half days a year – bringing the total up to 440 half days or 220 working days a year – provincial stipendiary magistrates are engaged in judicial duties other than sitting in court. This represents the better part (0.8) of one day per week over a 44-week working year and means that in practice most provincial stipendiaries are typically sitting in court for four rather than five days a week.

The picture for London is clearer because systematic records are kept by the office of the Chief Metropolitan Magistrate. The records show the 47 London stipendiaries undertaking an average of approximately 335 court sittings per year (approximate, because it is not clear to what extent court sittings are undertaken on days when training and other activities are scheduled for only a morning or afternoon). If training, meetings and other approved judicial duties are added, this represents 186 working days per annum. Which is to say that London stipendiaries currently sit in court rather less, on average, than their provincial colleagues.

The information gathered from the stipendiary magistrates' diaries, recorded for the same period as the lay magistrates' diaries, confirms this overall picture. If Bank and annual holidays are excluded, the stipendiary magistrates' diaries suggest that during a normal five-day working work most stipendiary magistrates sit in court for on average eight sessions per week, mornings or afternoons.

2.9   THE TYPES OF CASES WHICH LAY AND STIPENDIARIES HANDLE

The official LCD policy on stipendiary magistrates is that though they may be drafted in to assist courts outside their commission areas to deal with sensitive cases (for example, the indictment of a local police officer or councillor), prolonged appearances (for example, trials expected to last more than three days) or legally complex proceedings (for example, high profile committal proceedings involving a large number of co-defendants), when sitting on their home patch they routinely handle, or should be handling, broadly the same range of cases as is heard by lay magistrates.

A prevalent unofficial view is almost exactly the opposite. This is that whether sitting in court at home or away, stipendiary magistrates generally deal with the 'heavy business'. Which is to say, that in the minds of critical lay magistrates, stipendiaries asset-strip court lists by having allocated to them the more serious and interesting cases, leaving the routine and intrinsically less demanding business (prosecutions for TV licence evasion, summary motoring cases, and so on) to their lay colleagues. Only in Inner London, where there are large numbers of stipendiaries and where the majority of court appearances may be heard by stipendiaries, is it said that this division of labour does not apply. In London, stipendiary and lay magistrates are said to operate almost in parallel with one another, whereas in the provinces the relationship is more one of a division of labour, complementary or otherwise, depending on one's viewpoint (see Seago et al., 1995, Chapter Four).

What light does the evidence shed on these competing portrayals? We gathered information from five sources: sessional data from the six participating courts with stipendiaries; observational data from the same courts; discussions with the clerks for the same courts about case allocation; analysis of the computerised court registers for two of the participating courts with stipendiaries; and a telephone survey of clerks for all courts with stipendiaries outwith the sample about case allocation policy.

The core data on which our comparison of lay and stipendiary magistrates' court work is based are derived from observations of court appearances. The observations were carried out in April and May 2000. Because our observers were able to observe only a sample of appearances in each of the ten participating courts, we asked the clerks to the justices to supply us with details as to how many courts sat during the six week period April 10 to May 27 and how those court sessions were allocated, by type of case, to stipendiary and lay magistrates. Though four out of the ten courts had no full-time stipendiary, it was technically possible for them to allocate work to a visiting full or part-time stipendiary, and two courts did so.

The picture that emerges from these sessional data (see Figure 2.9) suggests that only in Inner London do stipendiaries handle routine summary matters and that elsewhere their caseload is slanted towards 'heavy business'. In the six courts with one or more full-time stipendiaries, the stipendiaries reportedly dealt with: only nine out of the 80 court sessions (11%) described as predominantly summary motoring (the nine sessions were all in the Inner London court where three-quarters of such sessions were dealt with by stipendiaries); 23 out of 150 sessions (15%) described as predominantly non-motoring summary cases; 418 out of 1,934 sessions (22%) described as 'mixed adult court business'; but 202 out of 435 sessions (46%) described as 'adult court – all or predominantly indictable'.

Figure 2.9

Allocation of court sessions to lay and stipendiary magistrates in sample courts

	Total	Adult court – all or mainly summary motoring	Adult court – all or mainly summary non-motoring	Adult court - all or mainly indict-able	Adult court mixed bus.	Youth court	Family court	Licensing court	Fines / Council tax
Rural 1									
- Lay	106	0	0	0	84	14	6	2	0
- Stipe (0 full time)	0	0	0	0	0	0	0	0	0
Rural 2									
- Lay	65	0	6	12	38	10	6	3	0
- Stipe (0 full time)	2	0	0	0	2	0	0	0	0
Mixed urban-rural									
- Lay	120	0	0	0	102	7	10	1	0
- Stipe (2 full time)	13	0	0	0	13	0	0	0	0
Urban 1									
- Lay	250	49	21	100	27	24	11	7	11
- Stipe (0 full time)	12	0	0	12	0	0	0	0	0
Urban 2									
- Lay	315	0	0	0	248	31	31	5	0
- Stipe (0 full time)	0	0	0	0	0	0	0	0	0
Urban 3									
- Lay	734	0	57	73	351	170	56	27	0
- Stipe (2 full time)	88	0	5	33	45	5	0	0	0
Metropolitan 1									
- Lay	873	53	33	0	466	184	120	17	0
- Stipe (3 full time)	192	0	12	0	174	5	1	0	0
Metropolitan 2									
- Lay	926	0	0	0	658	129	127	12	0
- Stipe (3 full time)	149	0	0	0	123	14	12	0	0
Outer London									
- Lay	257	15	37	42	88	54	18	3	0
- Stipe (1 full time)	51	0	6	21	17	6	1	0	0
Inner London									
- Lay	233	3	0	118	11	96	0	5	0
- Stipe (5 full time)	259	9	0	148	46	56	0	0	0
Total lay	3,879	120	154	345	2,073	719	385	82	11
Total stipendiary	766	9	23	214	420	86	14	0	0

Source: Justices' clerks' records

It was originally intended that the electronic court registers for the ten participating courts should be analysed for the same periods. In the event, this proved technically possible in only two of the courts, both large provincial urban courts with full-time stipendiaries. The results of the court register analysis for these two courts (see Figure 2.10) show that though the allocational pattern differs somewhat – stipendiaries in Urban Court 3 deal with proportionately more of the serious cases and proportionately fewer of the more minor cases than stipendiaries in Metropolitan Court 2 – nevertheless the allocation of work to stipendiaries is much more evenly distributed than the sessional data suggest. With the exception of fines enforcement and private prosecutions, the stipendiary magistrates appear to deal, in these two large provincial courts at least, with the full range of criminal cases, including summary cases, both motoring and non-motoring. It is apparent that in Urban Court 3 and Metropolitan Court 2, sessions described as 'Adult court, mixed business' include a good many summary motoring and summary non-motoring cases.

Figure 2.10

Case heard by lay and stipendiary magistrates in two sample courts

	Metropolitan 2		Urban 3	
	Lay %	Stipe %	Lay %	Stipe %
Violence/sex	83	17	75	25
Robbery	87	13	69	31
Burglary	82	18	62	38
Drugs	75	25	64	36
Dec/theft/criminal damage	78	22	72	28
Other indictable	77	23	63	37
Summary non-motoring	84	16	74	26
Summary motoring	65	35	80	20
Private prosecutions	100	0	98	2
Breach of court orders	84	16	68	32
Amend of bail conditions	78	22	68	32
Fines enforcement	100	0	100	0
All cases	75	25	76	24

Source: Court register electronic records held locally

The fact that stipendiaries hear most of the range of classes of offences does not necessarily mean, however, that they hear the same *types* of appearances relating to those classes of offences as lay magistrates. The clerks to the justices with whom we spoke, both those for the participating courts and others with stipendiaries, generally indicated that they allocated sensitive, legally or procedurally complex and prolonged cases to their stipendiaries and most reported that summary cases in which defendants were generally dealt with in their absence were seldom heard by the stipendiaries. In one or two instances the clerks also indicated that case allocation between lay and stipendiary magistrates was a difficult issue for them to manage. There were instances of individual stipendiaries stipulating that they did not wish to undertake certain types of work and of lay magistrates resenting the fact that they felt deprived of complex, and therefore interesting, cases that they felt perfectly capable of handling. There was occasional reference to accountability difficulties. Could the clerk tell a resistant stipendiary what cases he or she would hear? Could the clerk determine when different stipendiary magistrates should take their holidays to ensure satisfactory stipendiary cover? Are stipendiaries accountable to the clerk and MCC locally, or to the LCD centrally?

These difficulties were not commonplace, but the survey of clerks tended to suggest that there were more significant differences in the allocation of cases between lay and stipendiary magistrates than the sessional data for the six participating courts, and the court register analysis for two of the courts, indicate. Furthermore, it became clear that different clerks adopt different practices when it comes to allocating lists to their stipendiaries. Some devise lists for the purpose.

Others do not: the stipendiary or stipendiaries are simply allocated one of the court lists that his or her lay colleagues might have taken. Where special stipendiary lists are drawn up, they tend to include more cases than the clerk considers a lay panel could have handled in the time available.

On one issue, however, all our sources of information are consistent. It is very rare for stipendiaries to sit with their lay colleagues. In only three out of 535 court sessions observed during our fieldwork did stipendiaries sit with lay colleagues: our survey of court clerks suggests that this figure almost certainly exaggerates the degree to which mixed panels hear cases.

Our conclusion, therefore, is that there are significant variations between courts with regard to the allocation of cases between stipendiary and lay magistrates. To suggest, as some lay magistrates do, that stipendiaries only undertake 'heavy business' is patently an exaggeration. The evidence suggests that both in London and the provinces most stipendiaries hear the full range of offences and types of appearances with the exception, in many provincial courts, of specialist fines enforcement and prosecution courts and summary motoring offences with guilty pleas taken in defendants' absence. This means, however, that most stipendiaries do tend to hear the more complex (which does not necessarily mean the more serious) cases, and these are by definition the more interesting. It is also clear that the management of lay and stipendiary magistrates' relations is sometimes difficult and that some clerks consider that these difficulties have hitherto not received, prior to the national integration of stipendiary magistrates at least, sufficient attention on the part of the LCD.

2.10 ARGUMENTS FOR AND AGAINST GREATER RELIANCE ON STIPENDIARY MAGISTRATES: THE MAGISTRATES' VIEWS

Suffice it to say that the allocation of court business between lay and stipendiary magistrates is a matter for policy. Future policy will, however, be constrained, in the short-term at least, by the expectations of present practitioners. In the questionnaire sent to all lay and stipendiaries we asked both types of magistrate, without prompting them with a list of answers, what, in their judgement, 'were the arguments, if any, for and against a greater reliance on stipendiary magistrates than is currently the case?'.

There is a marked contrast in the views of lay and stipendiary magistrates on this question (see Figure 2.11). Over half (55%) of lay magistrates do not suggest any arguments in favour of having more stipendiaries. One-third (33%) specifically say that there are no advantages. All stipendiaries mention advantages. The two principal advantages mentioned by both groups are, however, the same: stipendiaries are considered to be faster or more efficient (56% of stipendiaries and 22% of lay magistrates) and they know the law better (48% of stipendiaries and 11% of lay magistrates).

Figure 2.11

Magistrates' arguments for a greater reliance on stipendiary magistrates

	Stipe	Lay magistrates						
	Total	Total	Court area type			Age		
			Lon-don	Urban	Rural	Under 45	45-64	65+
Base	27	1,120	126	832	162	123	814	173
	%	%	%	%	%	%	%	%
Faster/efficient/quicker systems	56	22	22	21	27	22	22	21
Skills to know the law better	48	11	11	12	8	12	12	9
Better for longer cases – lasting several days	15	9	6	10	6	5	9	16
Complicated legal issues	33	9	5	10	6	8	8	12
Nothing	–	33	32	32	40	31	33	33
Not stated	–	23	23	23	20	24	23	20

Base: All respondents
Source: Magistrates' questionnaires

Figure 2.12 shows that two-thirds (63%) of stipendiaries cite no arguments against greater reliance on stipendiaries. This applies to only 18 per cent of lay magistrates. The main arguments raised by lay magistrates is that it is better to have magistrates from all walks of life (37%) and that it is unfair to have only one person sitting in judgement on a defendant (35%) – an argument with which, interestingly, 11 per cent of stipendiaries agree.

Figure 2.12

Magistrates' arguments against a great reliance on stipendiary magistrates

	Stipe	Lay magistrates						
	Total	Total	Court area type			Age		
			Lon-don	Urb-an	Rural	Under 44	45–64	65+
Base	27	1,120	126	832	162	123	814	173
	%	%	%	%	%	%	%	%
Better to have magistrates from all walks of life	-	37	35	38	35	43	38	32
Unfair to have only one person sitting in judgement	11	35	46	35	21	27	37	32
Lack of knowledge of personal circumstances	15	22	20	21	37	18	25	14
Less representative of the local people	4	19	26	17	21	24	19	13
Financial	-	13	7	12	21	16	13	8
Nothing	44	5	6	5	4	6	5	9
Not stated	19	13	7	13	11	12	11	17

Base: All Respondents
Source: Magistrates' questionnaires

However, lay magistrates who sit on benches with stipendiaries are less likely than their colleagues who sit on benches without stipendiaries to say it is unfair to have one person sitting in judgement

(19% compared to 36%), though they are more likely to say that it is fairer to have magistrates from all walks of life (37% compared to 29%). It is significant that a small minority of stipendiaries (15%) agree that an argument *against* having more stipendiaries is that they are more likely than lay magistrates to lack knowledge about the personal circumstances of defendants.

In conclusion, it is apparent to us from other sources (bench meetings, conversations with individual magistrates and their clerks) that many lay magistrates are wary of what they see as the asset-stripping consequences of employing stipendiaries. Why, they ask, should they volunteer to give so much of their unpaid time to this public office if they are deprived of the opportunity to hear interesting cases likely to engage their intelligence? By the same token, stipendiary magistrates think it odd if their legal expertise is not exploited by allocating to them the most legally and procedurally demanding cases in which serious decisions must be made. In Chapter Seven we shall see that in other jurisdictions there are examples of either lay and stipendiary magistrates hearing what we may term the more run-of-the-mill cases that can be dealt with relatively mechanically. This does not mean, however, that such a policy could be adopted in England and Wales without upsetting the expectations of magistrates, both lay and stipendiary, whose recruitment and commitment has been established on a different basis.

3 MAGISTRATES' WORKING METHODS AND DECISIONS

3.1 THE RESEARCH OBJECTIVE AND THE DATA COLLECTION METHOD

The focus of this study concerns the manner in which lay and stipendiary magistrates undertake their core task – dealing with criminal cases in the adult and youth courts. Our aim is to establish whether there are differences in the way stipendiary and lay magistrates deal with criminal cases and, to the extent that there are differences, to examine their cost and other consequences.

From late April until early June 2000 we employed observers to sit in a sample of courts at the ten participating magistrates' courts. Targets were set for the observation of different types of court sessions heard by lay and stipendiary magistrates (in those six courts where there were stipendiaries) so that most types of appearances – first appearances, adjourned proceedings, trials, cases adjourned for sentencing, and so on – and most aspects of magistrates' criminal jurisdiction were covered. The observers were trained to look at many aspects of proceedings and to record, using pen technology, the details on a pre-programmed lap-top computer (for methodological details, see Appendix B). At the end of every day each observer was required to transmit the recorded data electronically to the central research office so that advice could be given regularly by the central research team about the selection of subsequent court sessions for observation. This method also enabled the central research team continuously to monitor the performance of each observer.

A premium was placed on gathering a robust set of observations of all the key criminal court decisions – whether to grant bail or remand in custody, whether to adjourn, whether to commit cases to the Crown Court, whether to acquit or find guilty, how to sentence, and so on. It was therefore decided to focus on court appearances in criminal cases of moderate seriousness, that is, the so-called either-way offences. The rationale was that any differences in the policies of lay and stipendiary magistrates regarding the more straightforward business of the magistrates' court – for example, summary motoring and non-motoring offences, private prosecutions by the Television Licensing Authority, and so on – would be revealed through electronic analysis of the court register.

Though court registers do not record the time taken for individual appearances, such cases are typically dealt with in large batches, in a high proportion of such cases offenders plead guilty by post and are invariably dealt with by way of fines. Since the average duration of court sessions would be known from the observational data, it would therefore be possible to gauge whether such cases were dealt with more rapidly or decided differently by lay and stipendiary magistrates in different courts.

This data collection plan unfortunately proved only partly realisable in practice. Different magistrates' courts employ several different IT systems for the recording of court appearances and these different systems are typically modified locally. There is no single coding system which can be applied universally to computerised locally-held magistrates' court register data: a coding system has to be designed to capture each system. Moreover, the systems are designed for purposes other than those for which we wished to employ them and thus certain information essential to our analysis – whether the court is presided over by lay or stipendiary magistrates, for example – is in many centres not recorded. Thus, whereas it was planned that court registers for not just the ten participating courts but a good many others would be transferred to the central research office and analysed electronically, in fact it proved possible, following several failed attempts, to do this for only two of the participating courts – Metropolitan 2 and Urban 3 – and one other without a stipendiary appointment. This data collection disappointment has made less robust the conclusions to which we can come. We shall refer to these difficulties and limitations as and when necessary.

3.1.1 The Observation Sample

A total of 535 court sessions (mornings or afternoons) was observed, 402 presided over by lay magistrates, 130 presided over by stipendiaries and three presided over by mixed panels of stipendiaries sitting with lay magistrates. Eighty per cent of lay panels comprised three magistrates, 16 per cent two magistrates, three per cent one magistrate and one per cent four magistrates. Observation targets were set for appearances of different types and these were broadly achieved. A breakdown of the sessions and types of appearances observed, by magistrates' court and type of magistrate presiding, is provided in Figures A.7 to A.9 in Appendix A.

On the basis of published Home Office court statistics regarding the numbers of defendants dealt with by each of the participating courts during 1998, and calculations based on surveys of adjournments and appearances per case (Mahoney, 2000), we have estimated the relationship between our appearance observation sample and the overall workload of the participating courts and that of courts nationally (see Figure 3.1).

The profile of cases in the courts in which observations took place is biased towards indictable cases at the expense of both summary motoring and non-motoring cases.

3.2   THE TIME TAKEN TO DEAL WITH COURT APPEARANCES

The quality of lay and stipendiary magistrates' performance being equal, the single most important potential difference between the two groups is the speed with which they deal with court business. If stipendiaries are quicker than lay magistrates – as common sense suggests they should be (stipendiaries have legal expertise which they can apply without receiving advice and if they sit alone they do not have to consult colleagues before reaching decisions), and as they are said to be (a belief widely held by both magistrates and justices' clerks (see Chapter Two) and regular court users (see Chapter Four)) – this has implications for the amount of time that everyone spends in court and, ultimately, the number of courtrooms which are needed. However, the issue as to how quickly court business is dealt with is complex, quite apart from questions of quality of decision-making and the perceptions of court participants. It involves more than simply establishing how much time is taken to deal with individual cases/appearances.

We have adopted two measures of speed. Firstly, the number of appearances dealt with per court session and secondly, the time taken to deal with individual appearances of different types. Both measures show unequivocally that stipendiary magistrates deal with more court appearances, and deal with those appearances faster, than do panels of lay magistrates. There are variations in the speed differential, but they are all in the same direction.

3.2.1 The Length of Court Sessions

The average court session, either a morning or afternoon, is 150 minutes – which in most courts means 10.00 – 12.30 or 14.00 – 16.30. There is only a small difference in the average duration of court sessions between lay and stipendiary magistrates (152 and 146 minutes respectively). Moreover, though there is variation between courts, and between stipendiaries and lay magistrates within courts, there is no clear pattern to the variations. Two of the smaller rural courts have the shortest and the longest average duration (124 and 168 minutes) and whereas stipendiaries' sessions are longer than those of their lay colleagues in one metropolitan court (171 minutes compared to 155 minutes) they are considerably shorter in the Inner London court (131 minutes compared to 162 minutes). It has previously been suggested that Inner London may generate insufficient work to support the lay bench and the number of stipendiary appointments there (see Seago et al., 1995, 19).[1]

Figure 3.1

Relationship between magistrates' courts workloads and the observation data

NATIONAL Annual data	Defendants	Appearances per defendant	Total appearances	Percentage of total appearances
Indictable	510,000	3.2	1,630,000	38
Summary non-motoring	590,000	1.8	1,060,000	25
Summary motoring	850,000	1.9	1,615,000	37
Total	–	–	4,305,000	
OBSERVED COURTS Annual data				
Indictable	74,000	3.2	236,800	47
Summary non-motoring	67,000	1.8	120,600	24
Summary motoring	76,000	1.9	144,400	28
Total	–	–	501,800	
OBSERVATIONS				
Indictable	–	–	–	83
Summary non-motoring	–	–	–	6
Summary motoring	–	–	–	11

Sources: Observation data; LCD Information Bulletin. Issue 3, 2000; Home Office Criminal Statistics

3.2.2 The Number of Appearances per Court Session

The average number of appearances by defendants of all types across all types of courts is 10.4 per court session. The figures for courts presided over by panels of lay magistrates and stipendiaries sitting alone is 10.1 and 11.8 respectively. If the length of court sessions is standardised at 150 minutes, the figures are 10.0 and 12.2 respectively. That is, stipendiaries deal with 22 per cent more appearances per court session of equal length. There were too few

---

[1] However since Seago's study, the Stipendiary Bench has reduced from 53 to 45, six court houses have closed and one PSA has been abolished.

observations of mixed tribunals (comprising a stipendiary and lay magistrates) to establish whether they conformed more to the stipendiary alone or lay magistrates pattern.

The speed differentials between lay magistrates and stipendiaries varies between courts, but the pattern everywhere is the same. Stipendiaries always deal with more appearances than their lay colleagues in the equivalent time.

3.2.3 Factors Relating to Speed of Progress: Retirements, Breaks and Efficiency

Three factors explain the more rapid progress of stipendiaries:

- unlike lay magistrates, stipendiaries very seldom retire during cases and when they do retire they do so for much less time than their lay colleagues
- stipendiaries process evidence and make decisions generally more rapidly
- there are fewer breaks in stipendiary court proceedings.

However, there is a limiting factor to stipendiaries' greater efficiency – the routine delay *between* cases, which is similar for stipendiaries and lay magistrates.

We shall consider each of these factors in turn.

By a break in proceedings we mean that the court temporarily rises *during* a session and *between* appearances because of some unforeseen event – for example, a magistrate realises that he or she knows a defendant or witness and another magistrate has to be found, or cases collapse and business has to be transferred from another court, or a case cannot proceed because a defence lawyer is currently appearing in an adjacent courtroom.

By a retirement we mean that the magistrates leave the court *during* an appearance in order to consider some evidence (to read a pre-sentence report, for example) or discuss a decision (whether to acquit or find the defendant guilty, for example).

However, even when all breaks and retirements are taken into account there remains a substantial amount of *unattributed* time not devoted to appearances, but falling between them. This is waiting time and is to some extent unavoidable. When waiting time is predictably going to be long, the magistrates may decide to rise and take a break. It is sensible, therefore to consider unattributed time and breaks together: in an average court session of two and a half hours, they account for 30 minutes, or 20 per cent of the time.

Whereas lay magistrates retire on 1.2 occasions per court session for an average of 16 minutes, stipendiary magistrates scarcely ever retire (0.2 occasions per session for an average of 3 minutes). However, when retirements are removed from the equation, stipendiary magistrates are still quicker (9 minutes per appearance compared to 10 minutes for lay magistrates).

Stipendiary magistrates are roughly half as likely to take breaks as their lay colleagues. That is, when there is some unforeseen delay, they tend to remain in court. However, if breaks are added to unattributed time, stipendiaries and lay magistrates perform similarly in terms of delay between cases – an average of three minutes per appearance.

Stipendiaries are nevertheless more time-efficient than their colleagues in two key respects: they retire less often and they deal with court business more speedily. Further, as we shall see, there is evidence that this greater efficiency is achieved while enquiring and challenging more than lay magistrates. We should also recall that it is likely that this greater speed is achieved in relation to cases which almost certainly include many that are more complex than those handled by lay colleagues.

Figure 3.2

Analysis of time budgets per session across ten courts

	Lay	Stipendiary
Session length	150 mins	150 mins
Time spent in appearances (excluding retirements)	102 mins	112 mins
Time spent in retirements	20 mins	1 min
Time spent in breaks between appearances	4 mins	2 mins
Unattributed time	24 mins	36 mins

Source: Observation data

Figures 3.2 and 3.3 show that, in total, stipendiaries spend more time dealing with appearances per session and less time in retirements. However, the greater number of appearances they handle results in more 'unattributed' time during a session. When calculated on an appearance basis, there is very little difference between lays and stipendiaries in the time spent in breaks or unattributed time. The stipendiaries gain by dealing with their appearances more quickly and by spending less time in retirements. Of the total time gained by stipendiaries per appearance, 32 per cent is accounted for by dealing with the business more quickly and 68 per cent by retiring less frequently and for shorter periods.

Figure 3.3

Analysis of time budgets per appearance across ten courts

	Lay	Stipendiary	Percentage to which stipendiaries are faster or (slower) than lays
Average number of appearances	10.0	12.2	
Time spent in appearances (excluding retirements)	10 mins	9 mins	9%
Time spent in retirements	2 mins	*	97%
Time spent in breaks between appearances	*	*	6%
Unattributed time	2 mins	3 mins	

Source: Observation data

* = less than 0.5 minutes

Parentheses indicate where stipendiaries are slower than lays

3.2.4 Speed by Bench Culture, Type of Appearance and Case

The fact that stipendiaries generally get through more court business per session than do lay magistrates does not of course mean that *all* stipendiaries are quicker than *all* lay magistrates or that they are faster at dealing with all types of cases and appearances. We do not have sufficient observations of particular panels of lay magistrates or particular stipendiaries to consider individual magisterial performance. But we are able to examine differences between benches and types of case.

The latter is a vital consideration when estimating the likely consequences of altering the balance between lay and stipendiary magistrates. For example, we hypothesise that when dealing with summary motoring cases, in a high proportion of which the defendant has pleaded guilty by post, there will be less of a time differential between lay magistrates and stipendiaries than for more complex matters such as indictable cases adjourned for sentence. This is likely because summary motoring cases are disposed of fairly mechanically according to an agreed tariff of financial penalties, are quite often heard by two rather then three lay magistrates, and are unlikely to cause lay magistrates to have to retire to discuss what decision to make. Support for this hypothesis is to be found in the fact that panels comprising two rather than three lay magistrates retire less often per session (0.8 compared to 1.3 occasions) and retire for shorter periods (12 compared to 17 minutes).

To the extent that there are different time differentials between types of appearances and cases, we need to get some picture of them in order to refine our estimates of the likely benefits of having

38

more stipendiaries within the system as a whole. Summary cases comprise a much larger proportion of overall magistrates' court business than they did in our observation sample.

In the same way that repeated examinations of decision-making between benches have shown substantial differences not attributable to case-mix (see Chapter One), so there appear also to be significant differences in the *efficiency* with which different benches handle court appearances due to the *manner* in which they deal with them.

If the length of court sessions is standardised to two and a half hours, then whereas the average number of appearances across all ten courts is 10.4, the range between benches is from 7.6 to 15.4 appearances. In only one court, Mixed Urban-Rural, do the stipendiaries not handle more appearances than their lay colleagues (see Figure 3.4). In the Mixed Urban-Rural court there is little difference between the two types of magistrate. This may be because in this court the stipendiaries share their time between several PSAs, which may mean that they hear cases that are significantly different in character from those heard by their lay colleagues.

There are striking differences between the benches in the degree to which the lay magistrates retire and the proportion of sessional time which is unattributable or consumed by breaks or the panels retiring. Whereas the average amount of time per session across all ten courts taken up by lay retirements is 16 minutes, the range between benches is from less than a minute (Inner London) to 42 minutes (Urban Court 2). Some benches have a culture of regularly retiring at some length, others rarely do so.

Equally striking are the differences in the amount of unattributable time per appearance in front of lay magistrates. This ranges from around one minute in most courts to nearly five minutes (Metropolitan 1) and over 11 minutes (Inner London).

The amount of lay bench sessional time which is unattributable or taken up by breaks ranges from 17 minutes (Mixed Urban-Rural, Urban 2 and Metropolitan 2) to 69 minutes (Inner London). The amount of lay bench sessional time absorbed by retirements, breaks and unattributable time ranges from 32 minutes (Mixed Urban-Rural) to 69 minutes (Inner London), or 21 and 46 per cent respectively of lay bench sittings.

In four of the six courts where there are stipendiary magistrates we find that stipendiary magistrates spend less time dealing with appearances than their lay colleagues. In one (Mixed Urban-Rural) they are apparently slower and in another (Metropolitan 1) the average time per appearance is the same. Also the total time spent in retirements, breaks and unattributed time is greater for lay magistrates than for stipendiaries in all but the Mixed Urban-Rural court.

Figure 3.4

Analysis of court time budgets

	Total	Rural 1	Rural 2	Mixed Urban-rural		Urban 1	Urban 2	Urban 3		Metropolitan 1		Metropolitan 2		Outer London		Inner London	
		Lay	Lay	Stipe	Lay	Lay	Lay	Stipe	Lay	Stipe	Lay	Stipe	Lay	Stipe	Lay	Stipe	Lay
Base: Sessions observed	535	40	52	10	33	49	53	21	49	15	44	22	34	21	36	40	12
Appearances per 150 minute sessions	10.4	6.9	10.0	12.1	12.5	9.1	7.7	14.3	8.4	11.2	8.9	14.3	9.4	10.9	8.0	9.2	5.7
Average time spent in appearances excluding retirements (mins)	106	108	102	115	118	117	91	120	91	108	89	118	113	122	117	106	81
Average time spent in retirements (mins)	14	23	27	2	15	12	42	3	35	*	15	3	20	0	15	*	1
Average time in breaks and unattributed (mins)	30	19	21	33	17	21	17	27	24	42	46	29	17	28	19	44	69
Retirements, breaks and unattributed time (mins)	44	42	48	35	32	33	59	30	59	42	62	32	37	28	34	44	69
Average time per appearance (excl retirements)	10	16	10	10	9	13	12	8	11	10	10	8	12	11	15	12	14
Breaks and unattributed time per appearance	3	3	2	3	1	2	2	2	3	4	5	2	2	3	2	5	12
Breaks, unattributed time and retirements per appearance	4	6	5	3	3	4	8	2	7	4	7	2	4	3	4	5	12

Source: Observation data

* = a number or percentage < 0.5

Moreover, most stipendiaries are more efficient, according to all these measures, than lay magistrates on benches other than their own. The exceptions are the stipendiaries in the Inner London court, whose unattributable time per case is relatively high and whose appearances heard per session rate is correspondingly low. It follows, conversely, that lay magistrates are generally less productive than stipendiaries elsewhere. The exception is the lay bench at the Mixed Urban-Rural court who achieve high appearance-per-session rates, retire relatively seldom and briefly, and whose unattributable time per-appearance rate is superior to that achieved by their own stipendiary and that of stipendiaries in four of the five other courts who have stipendiaries. It is not clear to what extent these outlier cases are examples of singular efficiency and inefficiency, or are the product of idiosyncratic case-mixes or case allocations.

If stipendiaries are more efficient at dealing with court business, are they more efficient at handling all types of appearances and to the same degree? The observational data suggest that though they handle all types of appearances more efficiently, the efficiency gains vary by type of appearance.

We hypothesised that the less mechanical the task, the more likely it would be that a panel of lay magistrates would have to retire. We also hypothesised that it was more likely that stipendiary magistrates would adopt a more inquisitorial approach than their lay colleagues. It is important to note that this inquisitorial/problem-solving dimension does not necessarily correspond with case seriousness. For example, a paper committal, as opposed to an 'old style' committal, of an indictable-only offence to the Crown Court by definition involves a serious matter, but it is an almost entirely mechanical task, which is one of the reasons why the Narey Report recommended (Home Office, 1997a, 35) that there no longer be a requirement that indictable-only offences begin life in the magistrates' court. Conversely, establishing, in the event of default, the rate at which a defendant fined for a summary offence should continue to pay his/her fine, often involves close questioning and examination of documentary evidence.

Thus, to take broad case categories, whereas stipendiaries are 27 per cent quicker with all types of triable-either-way crime appearances (an average of 10 minutes per appearance compared to 14 minutes), they are 33 per cent quicker when dealing with summary motoring appearances (5 minutes compared to 7 minutes) and 35 per cent quicker when dealing with summary non-motoring appearances (10 minutes compared to 15 minutes). The data suggest therefore that the time savings are marginally greater for summary appearances than the triable-either-way cases. This finding is contrary to our expectation. However, the differences are of a similar order of magnitude. We note later in this chapter that there is no reason to expect that the triable-either-way cases coming before stipendiaries and lay magistrates should be any different as regards their seriousness. Aggregating over all types of appearances, the like-for-like appearance data suggest that stipendiaries are around 30 per cent faster than lay magistrates in dealing with court business.

However, a focus on *types* of appearance within the arena of triable-either-way crime (see Figure 3.5) shows that, while the gain from having stipendiaries as opposed to lay magistrates handle paper committal, mode of trial and plea and directions hearings is insignificant, there are substantial gains to be reaped when they take first appearances where bail and custody decisions have to be made, conduct trials and hear cases previously adjourned for sentence (26%, 30% and 49% faster respectively). This finding is in accordance with our hypothesis that the greatest efficiency gains from employing stipendiaries arise when inquisition is most required and, we suggest, probably explains why the earlier comparison between the time taken for dealing with triable-either-way and summary cases generally was contrary to our expectations: the comparisons above failed to compare like-for-like appearances.

Figure 3.5

Average time taken per appearance (minutes) (including retirement time)

	Lay	Stipendiary	% that a stipendiary is faster (slower) than a lay[1]
First appearance	13	9	26%
Previously adjourned for sentence	24	12	49%
Plea and directions	10	10	(4%)
Mode of trial	12	12	7%
Intermediate hearing	12	9	31%
Full committal (6i)	17	15	6%
Paper committal (6ii)	6	8	(26%)
Trial	34	24	30%
Other previously adjourned	12	10	20%

Source: Observation data
[1] Percentages calculated on un-rounded data.

3.2.5 Speed and Effectiveness

The speed with which magistrates deal with court appearances is not, and should never be, the principal test of their effectiveness. If greater throughput of appearances involves injustice or discourtesy, or if parties to proceedings do not feel that they have been heard properly, then the court has not delivered the service it exists to provide. If victims, witnesses or defendants, and those whose task it is to represent their interests, leave the court dissatisfied or aggrieved then the purpose of the exercise has been undermined and the legitimacy of the criminal court system damaged. Moreover, short-term attempts to save time may be counter-productive. A magistrate who rejects an application from solicitors for time out of court briefly to consult with their warring clients in family proceedings may get the case started on time but may, by so doing, precipitate a prolonged and damaging court battle which might otherwise have been avoided through the construction of a mutually agreed settlement. Likewise, a magistrate who gives insufficient time to the investigation and construction of a sensible bail arrangement, or who fails adequately to inquire into the ability of a defendant to pay a financial penalty, may be creating problems which will ultimately absorb the time and resources of not just the court but the police and other agencies. It is vital, therefore, that we consider whether there is any evidence of a downside to what appears to be the greater effectiveness of stipendiaries.

We have looked for such evidence by a variety of means. We asked our observers to record whether questions were asked by the bench of the defence or prosecution in certain circumstances, whether decisions were explained to the parties to the proceedings and, following the criteria by which lay magistrates appraise each other's performance, whether the magistrate was courteous, attentive, appropriately sympathetic, and so on. These data are discussed below. We also interviewed a large number of regular court users and sought their opinions about the performance of the two types of magistrates: this evidence is discussed in Chapter Four. Finally, we conducted a large scale public opinion survey, one-third (32%) of the respondents to which said they had attended a magistrates' court either as a defendant, victim, witness, or in some other capacity: we discuss the findings from this survey in Chapter Five.

None of the evidence gathered under these headings leads us to conclude that, as the magistrates' courts system operates today, there is a downside to the greater effectiveness which stipendiaries demonstrate in terms of the speed with which they deal with cases. Indeed, the reverse is the case. Stipendiary magistrates emerge with credit from all these other measures of effectiveness.

It must be recognised however, that to the extent that the credibility of magistrates' courts rests on the participation of lay persons, or decision-making by panels (which at this level must mean the continued involvement of lay persons), then the corollary is that proceedings will necessarily be slower. Lay persons must be legally advised and members of panels must consult with one another before making decisions. Both processes take time.

3.3   ASSESSING THE QUALITY OF LAY AND STIPENDIARY MAGISTRATES' WORK

We have attempted to assess the quality of magistrates' performance without trespassing on issues of rectitude or justice in decision-making (see Chapter One). What follows must be read with one word of caution in mind: we do not know what effect the presence of our observers may have had on the behaviour of the magistrates they observed. We doubt the effect is great, but it is likely that there was some. The presence in the courthouse of our observers for several weeks was generally made known to the bench and we know that in at least one case, magistrates were advised by their Clerk and Chairman that they should exhibit model behaviour during this period. However, our observers were a discreet presence within courtrooms: it is unlikely that individual magistrates remained so conscious of them that their normal pattern of behaviour was greatly altered.

3.3.1 The Observers' Assessments

In one respect the quality of stipendiaries sitting alone and lay magistrates sittings as panels cannot be compared. By convention, magistrates not chairing the court (the winger or wingers) are required to put any questions they may have through the chairman. In only 12 instances during 3,921 appearances did our observers record a winger asking a question of, or making a comment to, any other person in court. Good chairing requires establishing whether colleagues have questions which they wish to be put and consulting colleagues regarding their views before reaching and announcing decisions. Team working is a key aspect of lay magistrate training and chairman appraisal. The evidence suggests that this courtesy and skill is almost always visibly exercised: in 98 per cent of appearances our observers judged that chairmen appeared to encourage participation from wingers.

The other performance criteria which observers were asked to apply are as applicable to stipendiaries sitting alone as lay panels (too few mixed panels were observed to make an assessment). The evaluations are subjective (see Appendix B1) but in practically all respects our observers judged that both lay and stipendiary magistrates scored almost uniformly well on all the criteria we asked them to apply on those occasions when the criteria were judged applicable (attentiveness is always applicable, whereas the ability to deal with unruly defendants is seldom called for) (Figure 3.6). That is, both lay and stipendiary magistrates:

- are attentive
- use non-jargon language which is easy to understand
- demonstrate a non-prejudicial attitude
- speak clearly and concisely
- ask questions where appropriate
- address defendants and other parties with courtesy
- ensure that everyone understands pronouncements.
-

On the other criteria both types of magistrates also score generally well, but stipendiaries score better. Stipendiaries are slightly more likely to:

- show command over proceedings
- provide clear and concise reasons for decisions.
- require explanation from those court participants who cause delay

The dimensions 'show appropriate concern for distressed parties' and 'deal effectively with unruly defendants or witnesses' were relatively rare events and did not provide an adequate basis for the comparison of lay and stipendiary magistrate performances: the base sizes were 66 and 13 appearances in front of lay and stipendiary magistrates respectively where there were distressed parties and 64 and 42 respectively where there were unruly defendants or witnesses. Also rare were cases where there was need to seek explanation from someone who had caused delay (274 for lay magistrates and 117 for stipendiary magistrates) and appearances where there were wingers for a stipendiary to consult (114). In other cases we have in excess of 2,000 appearances in front of lay magistrates and in excess of 900 in front of stipendiaries on which to base our conclusions.

These findings are generally consistent with those derived from the court users' survey (see Chapter Four). Regular court users (solicitors, CPS personnel, probation officers, and so on) think that lay magistrates are slightly better at using simple language, showing concern for distressed victims, and being courteous. But they think that stipendiaries are generally better when it comes to demonstrating command over court proceedings, explaining decisions so that defendants understand, dealing effectively with incidents of unruliness, requiring explanations for delay, and those other aspects of performance which derive from confidence. What the observation data suggest is that, in fact, lay magistrates generally perform well on all these criteria also. Of course, the few occasions when individual lay magistrates fail to exercise command or do not deal with incidents appropriately – and the regular court users say that there is, not surprisingly, greater variation in the performance of individual lay than stipendiary magistrates – almost certainly undermines the reputation of the lay magistracy overall.

Figure 3.6

Qualitative assessment of magistrates' performance across ten courts*

	Lay	Stipendiary
	%	%
Appear to be attentive	100	100
Use simple language without jargon	100	100
Demonstrate a non-prejudicial attitude	100	100
Speak clearly and concisely	99	100
Ask questions that are appropriate	99	100
Show courtesy to the defendant	99	99
Show courtesy to other court members	99	99
Address defendant in appropriate manner	99	99
Encourage participation from wingers / flankers	98	100
Ensure all understand pronouncements	97	98
Show command over proceedings	96	100
Provide clear and concise reasons for decisions	95	99
Show appropriate concern for distressed parties	93	91
Deal effectively with unruly defendants / witnesses	83	97
Require explanation from those who cause delay	71	95

Base: All appearances (excluding 'not applicable')

* % saying quality was displayed

Source: Observation data

3.3.2 Indicators of Magisterial Command Over Proceedings

Our brief interviews with regular court users did not enable us to discover the basis on which they came to their conclusions regarding the relative merits of lay and stipendiary magistrates. But by getting our court observers to record a wealth of detail of how the thousands of court appearances were handled by lay and stipendiary magistrates, it is possible to establish indicators almost certainly picked up on by regular court users. Five examples have been outlined in Figure 3.7.

Stipendiary hearings are more questioning and challenging. Furthermore, the questions are much more likely to be put by the magistrate than by the court's legal advisor. The observational data show conclusively that whereas stipendiaries run their own show, lay magistrates rely heavily on their legal advisors to probe or challenge.

Lay magistrates, like their stipendiary colleagues, make the key announcements. At initial hearings, when bail/custody decisions have to be made and announced, at trials when the tribunal's verdict has to be communicated, and when passing sentence, the announcements and, if stated, the justifications for the decisions, are almost always uttered exclusively by the magistrates, lay or stipendiary. However, when it comes to explaining what decisions mean – the terms of the bail decision or the meaning of the sentence – the explanations, though normally provided by the magistrates, are, in a minority of cases at lay magistrates' hearings, provided by the magistrates' legal advisor. This almost never happens at stipendiaries' hearings. Stipendiaries almost always explain decisions themselves. Thus, on those 1,040 observed occasions when the terms of a bail/custody decision were being explained, at stipendiary hearings it was done on 99 per cent of the occasions exclusively by the stipendiary compared to 94 per cent at lay magistrates' hearings.

Other procedural sequences illustrate the same difference. Questions during lay magistrates' hearings are often put by the court legal advisor, whereas stipendiaries almost invariably do the job themselves. Six examples are given in Figure 3.8 of specific actions required during court proceedings. The figures show the percentage of instances where the magistrate performed the action rather than another court member.

The differences between stipendiaries' and lay magistrates' hearings are striking if the observational data are summarised in terms of looking at the overall proportion of court appearances at which questions of any sort are put to the prosecution or the defence and, when questions are put, who puts them. It becomes clear why regular court users – prosecutors and lawyers in particular – say that they prepare more, and believe their colleagues prepare more, when appearing before stipendiaries as opposed to lay magistrates (see Chapter Four) – because they expect to be challenged more often.

Figure 3.7

Appearances during which there were questions or challenges from the bench across ten courts

	Lay	Stipendiary
Remand in custody/application of bail conditions		
- questions to the defence	40% (226)	56% (83)
- questions to the prosecution	24% (226)	48% (83)
Accused in custody, defence seeking release on bail		
- questions to the defence	31% (159)	58% (129)
Adjournment sought		
- adjournment challenged	8% (888)	13% (288)
Court to decide whether to accept jurisdiction in triable-either-way cases		
- questions from the bench	18% (300)	59% (141)

Base sizes for each percentage are shown in parentheses
Source: Observation data

Figure 3.8

Announcements made or questions put from the bench across ten courts

	Lay	Stipendiary
Announce adjournment decisions	96% (1,402)	99% (568)
Announce extension of legal aid or other provision	87% (265)	98% (173)
Seek advice from Probation Service regarding reports	82% (185)	83% (85)
Ask questions to establish the defendants' means	68% (230)	92% (94)
Ask questions to establish the defendants' circumstances other than their means	63% (157)	93% (117)
Correct the behaviour of persons in the public gallery	53% (31)	71% (28)

Base sizes for each percentage are shown in parentheses

Source: Observation data

It is clear from the observational data that persons appearing before stipendiaries stand a much greater chance of being questioned about what they have to say than is the case at lay magistrates' hearings (Figure 3.9). Moreover, whereas at stipendiaries' hearings the questions almost always come from the bench, at lay magistrates' hearings the fewer questions are almost as likely to come from the court legal advisor as the magistrates.

Asking questions is of course not self-evidently to be encouraged: it depends on whether the questions are sensible or not, whether applications deserve to be challenged and evidence probed. In the opinion of our observers, as we have seen, the questions that magistrates did ask seemed to them overwhelmingly to be appropriate. We did not ask our observers whether they thought more questions should have been asked: we did not consider it appropriate, in the same way that we considered it inappropriate to ask the observers to assess the justice or good sense of magistrates' decisions. Nevertheless the issue remains as to whether the differences in the *manner* in which lay and stipendiary magistrates conduct their proceedings is associated with differences in the *substance* of their decisions. It is to this issue that we turn now.

Figure 3.9

Questions put to prosecution and defence across ten courts

	Percentage appearances where occurred	By magistrate	By advisor	By both
		%	%	%
To prosecution				
- Lay	47	38	46	16
- Stipendiary	66	91	4	5
To defence				
- Lay	49	48	38	15
- Stipendiary	70	93	3	4

Source: Observation data

3.4   LAY AND STIPENDIARY MAGISTRATES: PATTERNS OF DECISION-MAKING

3.4.1 Introduction

Following the finding by Flood-Page and Mackie (1998, Chapter 7) that stipendiaries are more likely than their lay colleagues, all other known factors being equal, to impose custodial sentences, there are two questions to be addressed. Firstly, do there appear to be differences in the pattern of decisions made by lay and stipendiary magistrates? Secondly, to the extent that differences appear to exist, are the differences real, or are they a function of the differential case allocation between the two groups? Because we were unable to analyse most court registers (see discussion at the beginning of this chapter), and because court registers in any case provide only a superficial guide to the case allocation between lay and stipendiary magistrates, we are able to provide only tentative answers to the second question. We shall address the two questions in turn but, before doing so, we shall consider the general pattern of offence and offender characteristics in the observed stipendiary and lay justice appearances.

3.4.2 The Pattern of Offences and Offenders at Observed Appearances: Lay Magistrates and Stipendiaries

We noted in Chapter Two that the analysis of the court registers in two of the participating courts, with two and three full-time stipendiary magistrates respectively, demonstrated that the stipendiaries undertook, with the exception of specialist fines enforcement courts and private prosecutions, the full range of criminal court work including summary motoring and non-motoring cases. The clerks to the justices for most of the six participating courts with stipendiaries confirmed that they allocated to their stipendiaries controversial, procedurally difficult or legally complex cases as well as prolonged trials – that is, the sort of cases for which clerks in courts without stipendiaries might seek through the LCD the assistance of a stipendiary.

These cases apart, the stipendiaries' allocation was weighted towards the triable-either-way cases. There was no reason to expect, however, that in relation to any particular type of triable-either-way hearing – bail/custody initial hearings, adjourned hearings, cases adjourned for sentencing, and so on – the cases coming before stipendiaries and lay magistrates should be any different as regards their seriousness. Moreover, those cases which might specially be allocated to a stipendiary (a controversial matter involving a local councillor charged with a theft, for example, or a motoring case involving a complex point of law) would not necessarily be more serious.

We asked our observers to record as many offence and offender characteristics as were mentioned in open court (the observers did not have access to pre-sentence reports or other case papers). Close scrutiny of these characteristics shows that the observed appearances before lay and stipendiary magistrates are very similar as regards to:

- the broad categories of offences involved (violence, burglary, drugs, and so on), the types of offences within broad categories (common assault, actual bodily harm and grievous bodily harm within offences of violence, for example) and the relative seriousness of the particular offences involved (the value of the criminal damage or the property stolen, the *modus operandi* of the burglaries, the types of drugs involved, and so on)
- the number of defendants and the number of charges involved
- the proportions of defendants with previous convictions both generally and for the same offence, who are on bail or awaiting trial for another offence or are already subject to a court order
- the proportions of defendants who are homeless or living in temporary or hostel accommodation, who are unemployed or whose income comprises state benefits.

Figure A.10, Appendix A shows the profile of offences dealt with by lay and stipendiary magistrates in the observed sample.

It follows that the observation data corroborate what clerks to justices informed us about case allocation patterns. There is nothing to suggest that any differences in the decision-making patterns between lay and stipendiary magistrates regarding triable-either-way offences is likely to be attributable to the fact that they are dealing with more or less serious offences. Finally, it should be noted that the percentages below refer to the observed sample, which is not representative of all appearances: the percentages are not a guide, therefore, to the *overall* proportionate use of custody with regard to all cases decided in the magistrates' courts concerned.

3.4.3 Issuing Arrest Warrants

There were 320 observed occasions when defendants failed, without prior agreement, to attend court hearings. Stipendiary magistrates are more likely to respond to this situation than their lay colleagues by issuing an arrest warrant (70% compared to 56%).

3.4.4 Bail/Custody Decisions

There were 309 observed occasions when the magistrates had to make a decision whether to remand the defendant in custody or, if granting bail, to determine whether the bail should be conditional or unconditional. Stipendiary magistrates are more likely than their lay colleagues to remand defendants in custody (37% compared to 19%). Of those defendants granted bail, the same proportion are given unconditional bail by stipendiaries and lay magistrates (33% and 34% respectively).

There were 228 observed occasions when the accused was being held in custody and the defence applied for bail. Stipendiary magistrates are more likely than their lay colleagues to reject the application and remand again in custody (51% compared to 43%).

There is also a difference in the pattern of reasons given by stipendiary and lay magistrates for imposing bail conditions or remanding the defendant in custody. Lay magistrates are much more likely to cite the likelihood of the defendant's failure to attend (based upon the seriousness of the offence) as a ground for remanding in custody, whereas stipendiaries are more likely to cite the likelihood of further offences.

Figure 3.10

Tribunal decisions where defence was applying for bail across ten courts

	Lay	Stipendiary
Base:	226	83
	%	%
Tribunal decision		
Unconditional bail	26	20
Bail with conditions	51	43
Remand in custody	19	37
Remand in local authority care	1	–
Outcome not known	2	–

Source: Observation data

3.4.5 Adjournments

There were 1,190 observed appearances at which either the defence or the prosecution requested an adjournment. The overall figures suggest that stipendiaries are less likely than their lay colleagues to grant such requests (84% compared to 96%), though in most of the cases where stipendiaries refuse to grant an adjournment they agree to put the case down the list for the session or the day (Figure 3.11). This is an illustration of a potential advantage which stipendiaries have over lay magistrates. Stipendiaries are generally sitting throughout the day, whereas lay magistrates are not (see Chapter Two). It follows that those requests for adjournments which are made on the basis of a need to consult someone outside the court, or establish some fact or consult some document not immediately available, are much more readily met by stipendiaries granting a few hours to make further progress.

However, the apparent difference between stipendiaries and lay magistrates is substantially attributable to the practice in an outlier court (Metropolitan 1) in which the stipendiaries were considerably more likely than elsewhere to put the case down the list rather than adjourn. Across the other courts the differences were smaller but, on average, there remained a marginal difference in the likelihood of accessions to requests for adjournments (stipendiary 93%, lay 97%).

Because this is an important issue with considerable cost and other consequences for the criminal justice system, we explored it from other angles. In Chapter Four we report that regular court users say that they behave differently when appearing before stipendiaries compared to lay magistrates and they think their colleagues do also. They say that they prepare better for stipendiaries than lay magistrates because they expect to be more closely questioned and challenged. If this is the case then one consequence may be that lawyers and CPS caseworkers do not even apply for adjournments that they might pursue before lay magistrates. This hypothesis has previously been outlined but not tested (see NAO, 1999, paragraph 4.62).

Adjournments can be distinguished between those that proceed logically from a current decision (for example, the magistrates have decided that the case is too serious for them to deal with and must be committed for trial or sentence to the Crown Court, or the magistrates not having the defendant's driving licence, or a print-out of it from the DVLC, when they have decided to impose penalty points and need to know whether he or she is eligible for disqualification under the totting-up procedure) and those that depend on an application from the prosecution or defence that they will be better prepared if given further time.

We asked our observers to distinguish all adjournments on this basis. The percentage of all appearances (excluding Metropolitan 1 as an outlier) that follow logically is the same for lay magistrates and stipendiary magistrates (22%). However, the percentage of appearances where requests for adjournments are transparent to the observers is higher for lay magistrates (31%) than stipendiaries (25%).

It is apparent, therefore, that if the extreme case of Metropolitan Court 1 (where stipendiaries are very substantially more likely to resist adjournments) is excluded from the analysis, the proportion of appearances resulting in an adjournment is nevertheless significantly higher before lay magistrates than stipendiaries (52% compared to 45%). This is partly because stipendiaries are more resistant to applications for adjournment and partly because, presumably in anticipation of their greater resistance, fewer applications for adjournment are made to stipendiaries.

Figure 3.11

Profile of accessions to adjournments across nine courts*

	Lay	Stipendiary
	2,342	988
	%	%
Adjournment sought/proceeds logically	53	47
Appearances where adjournment transparently sought	31	25
Appearances adjourned (including proceed logically)	52	45
Percentage of accessions to requests for adjournments	97	93

Base: All criminal appearances

*Excludes outlier

Source: Observation data

There remains the issue of the length of adjournments granted, another important consideration when it comes to the key performance indicator of delay in completing court proceedings.

The data show that both adjournments requested and granted are marginally shorter on average at stipendiary compared to lay magistrates' hearings (Figure 3.12).

Figure 3.12

Duration of Adjournments requested and granted across ten courts

	Lay	Stipendiary
Duration of adjournment requested (days)	17.2	15.1
Duration of adjournment granted (days)	18.2	15.9

Source: Observation data

This is further evidence that, by one means or another, reductions in delay in court proceedings are probably better achieved by stipendiaries than lay magistrates.

3.4.6 Committals

There were 447 observed appearances when the magistrates, faced with triable-either-way offences which the defendants wished to be heard in the magistrates' court, but the prosecution thought suitable for the Crown Court, had to decide whether to accept jurisdiction of the case or commit to the Crown Court. There was little difference in the rate at which the two types of magistrate committed cases to the Crown Court (67% for stipendiaries compared to 65% for lay magistrates).

3.4.7 Trials

Our observers were asked to observe trials, but to avoid, on resource grounds, trials predicted to last beyond a single sitting. Trials are relatively unusual events in magistrates' courts so it was always apparent that there might be difficulty in securing a sufficient number of observations to say anything about any differences that might emerge between lay and stipendiary magistrates. In the event, sessions were selected in which 105 trials were due to take place, 24 presided over by stipendiaries and 81 by lay magistrates. However, 78 of these 105 projected trials collapsed following a prosecution decision to discontinue proceedings. In the event, therefore, there were too few observations (particularly of trials before stipendiaries) to permit any comparison between lay and stipendiary magistrates to be made.

3.4.8 Sentencing

There were 930 observed occasions on which the magistrates passed sentence. Stipendiaries are much more likely to use sentences higher up the tariff (25% of cases resulting in an immediate custodial sentence compared to 12% for lay magistrates, 12% of cases resulting in a probation order compared to 8%) and much less likely to use those lower down the range (8% and 28% for conditional discharges and fines, compared to 12% and 39%) (Figure 3.13). It is interesting to note that whereas stipendiaries use probation orders to a greater extent than their lay colleagues, the reverse is the case with community service orders and compensation orders (10% for lay magistrates and 7% for stipendiaries).

This pattern of more severe sentencing holds consistently for all six courts in which there are stipendiaries.

Figure 3.13

Sentences passed across the ten courts*

	Lay	Stipendiary
	643	287
	%	%
Immediate custody	12	25
Community service	10	7
Probation order	8	12
Fine	39	28
Conditional discharge	12	8
Compensation order	10	7
Costs	46	30
Disqualified from driving	14	11
Licence endorsed	11	8

Base: Appearances where sentence was passed

* Only sentences passed in 5% or more cases are listed

Source: Observation data

Figure 3.14

Sentences passed across ten courts by lay magistrates in courts with and without stipendiaries*

	Lays in courts with stipendiaries	Lays in courts without stipendiaries
	349	294
	%	%
Immediate custody	13	6
Community service	11	4
Probation order	8	9
Fine	39	40
Conditional discharge	10	21
Compensation order	9	11
Costs	47	40
Disqualified from driving	14	15
Licence endorsed	11	10

Base: Appearances where sentence was passed

* Only sentences passed in 5% or more cases are listed

Source: Observation data

3.4.9 Differences between the Decision-Making of Lay Magistrates in Courts with and without Stipendiaries

Stipendiary magistrates sometimes contribute to the training of lay magistrates and in some areas they very occasionally sit with them. Flood-Page and Mackie (1998, Chapter 7) suggest that the presence of stipendiaries might therefore be expected to exercise some influence over their lay colleagues and they find limited evidence to support this 'trickle down' hypothesis in relation to sentencing. They find that lay magistrates in courts with stipendiaries make proportionately greater use of custody than do lay magistrates in courts without stipendiaries. We tested the hypothesis in relation to each of the decisions discussed above.

In only two areas of decision-making are lay magistrates in courts with stipendiaries more likely to make decisions in accord with their stipendiary colleagues than are lay magistrates in courts without stipendiaries – resistance to adjournments and the tendency to sentence more severely. This is significant because these are the only two areas of decision-making in which stipendiaries are consistently different from their lay colleagues across all six of the participating courts with stipendiaries.

In relation to adjournments, lay magistrates in courts with stipendiaries are marginally less likely to accede to requests for adjournments compared to lay magistrates in courts without stipendiaries (95% compared to 97%). However, in relation to sentencing, lay magistrates in courts with stipendiaries are substantially more severe in their decisions than are magistrates elsewhere (Figure 3.14). They rely to a much greater extent on custodial sentences (13% compared to 6%) and conditional discharges much less (10% compared to 21%).

In relation to bail/custody decisions, however, magistrates in courts without stipendiaries are tougher than their colleagues in courts with stipendiaries (25% of cases remanded in custody compared to 17%). It is not clear to what degree this is because stipendiaries tend to deal with a higher proportion of cases in which this outcome is more likely.

3.5 THE IMPLICATIONS OF HAVING LAY OR STIPENDIARY MAGISTRATES FOR THE ROLE OF THE COURT LEGAL ADVISOR

In Chapter Six, when considering the cost implications of employing stipendiaries, we raise the question of whether there is a need for a legally qualified court legal advisor in court when a stipendiary is sitting. Stipendiaries currently enjoy the services of a legally qualified advisor and, in conversation, stipendiaries have told us that they value the service, though it has been suggested to us that it is an unnecessary luxury. In practice, as we have seen, whereas lay magistrates rely extensively on their court legal advisors to ask questions of the defence and prosecution and other court practitioners, stipendiaries tend overwhelmingly to undertake these tasks themselves. But are there other indicators of differential use of court legal advisors between stipendiary and lay magistrates?

Lay magistrates, as we have seen, are five times as likely to retire as stipendiaries. But the manner in which the two types of magistrates retire is also different. Whereas more than two-thirds (69%) of stipendiary retirements do not involve the court legal advisor at all, only one-third (37%) of lay magistrate retirements do not involve the clerk retiring at some stage with them. The usual pattern (54% of lay justice retirements) is for the magistrates to leave the court alone, and then to call for the legal advisor, who returns before the magistrates do. This is the approved practice, demonstrating the magistrates' independence, though whether it will survive the Human Rights Act is questioned: some commentators anticipate that the Human Rights Act will be interpreted so as to ensure that all legal advice given to lay magistrates is given in open court (Gibson, 1999).

Both lay and stipendiary magistrates regularly consult their legal advisors in open court, though not necessarily about legal matters. Lay magistrates consult their advisors more frequently than do stipendiaries (during 56% of appearances compared to 32%) (Figure 3.15).

Figure 3.15

Consultations with court legal advisor

	Lay	Stipendiary
	2,696	1,166
	%	%
Frequency of consultations		
Several occasions	9	2
Once or twice	46	30
No consultation observed	44	68

Base: All criminal appearances

Source: Observation data

Moreover, there is a difference in the manner in which stipendiaries and lay magistrates consult their legal advisors. Most advice is sought and given orally so that the advice can generally be heard, though this is more likely to be the case with stipendiaries (77% of occasions compared to 57%). Advice to lay magistrates is more often given in a whisper with the clerk standing to face the bench, either always or sometimes, than is the case with stipendiaries.

3.6 DIFFERENCES BETWEEN FREQUENTLY AND INFREQUENTLY SITTING LAY MAGISTRATES

We noted in Chapter Two that there are significant differences between individual magistrates within benches as to how often they sit in court. Since some lay magistrates are more practised than others, the question arises as to whether there are differences in their behaviour arising from this fact. When this proposition was put to the clerks to the justices for the ten participating courts, their view was that, though there are obviously differences in the manner in which individual lay magistrates chair courts, they did not think those differences to be systematically related to the frequency of sitting.

We tested the proposition by asking our court observers to record the name of the chairman of each court session presided over by lay magistrates and, on the basis of the sittings records obtained from the clerks, the panel was then classified as 'infrequent' (35 or fewer sittings per annum), 'average' (36 to 45 sittings inclusive) and frequent (over 45 sittings) sitters. This approach does not take into account the characteristics of the wingers (who may sit either more or less frequently than the chairman), but was adopted on the grounds of practical feasibility and the assumption that the chairman has the active role and sets the tone for the panel.

Analysis of the data relating to all the questions covered in this chapter reveals little in the way of patterned differences between frequent and infrequent sitters, but there are some differences.

Panels chaired by frequent sitters deal with more appearances per standardised court session than do panels chaired by average and infrequent sitters (10.5, 10.2 and 9.9 appearances per 150 minutes respectively). This appears partly to be attributable to the fact that panels chaired by infrequent sitters are more likely to retire (1.6 retirements per session, compared to 1.1 and 1.2 for average and frequent sitters).

The frequency with which panel chairmen sit is not related to any patterned differences in the decisions that panels make. However, frequently sitting chairmen are more likely to take responsibility, as opposed to leaving the task to the court legal advisor, for establishing defendants' means (73% compared to 52% and 55% for average and infrequent sitters) or establishing other aspects of their circumstances in the absence of reports (73% compared to 57% and 50%). Conversely, infrequent sitters are more likely visibly to consult their wingers (73% compared to 62% and 54%) and most likely to suffer corrections from the court legal advisor (7% compared to 5% and 4%). There is some support, therefore, for the proposition that more practised panel chairmen make fewer procedural errors and, presumably being generally more confident, tend to take the lead more in proceedings.

4 INSIDER OPINIONS ON LAY AND STIPENDIARY MAGISTRATES

The persons who know best the performance of lay and stipendiary magistrates are those who work with, support or appear before them in court on a regular basis – the 'insiders' as we shall call them. In this chapter we report what they have to say on the subject of lay and stipendiary magistrates, the differences between the two groups and whether these differences affect their own and other court users' behaviour.

4.1 METHODOLOGY

During the course of the observational fieldwork in the ten participating courts, we asked our court observers to note the names and contact details of persons appearing regularly in the court who might be suitable candidates for subsequent telephone interview. The court observers were instructed to gather roughly equal numbers of names of persons in five categories – court personnel (legal advisors and ushers), prosecutors (mostly CPS personnel but including local authority, Television Licensing Authority, Inland Revenue and other prosecuting officials), police officers and other professional witnesses, defence lawyers and probation officers, social workers and Victim Support co-ordinators – roughly 60 in all for each court. The list of approximately 600 names thus generated was used as the sampling frame from which to conduct telephone interviews with 400 regular court users. Further details of the methodology employed are given in Appendix B.

The breakdown of the targeted sample actually achieved is described in Figure 4.1. There are many more defence lawyers and fewer prosecutors, probation officers and social workers in the achieved sample than was aimed at: many more defence lawyers appeared to our observers to be regular court attenders and members of the latter groups subsequently proved elusive when it came to contacting them by telephone.

Figure 4.1

The sample of regular court users by court

	Court legal advisors and ushers	Police officers/ professional witnesses	Prosecutors	Defence lawyers	Probation officers/ social workers/ victim support
Total	82	75	43	145	56
Rural 1	5	9	6	15	5
Rural 2	8	4	2	12	2
Mixed urban-rural	0	5	1	15	4
Urban 1	4	9	7	11	5
Urban 2	9	4	3	1	11
Urban 3	20	12	8	28	10
Metropolitan 1	10	5	4	14	4
Metropolitan 2	12	4	6	19	9
Outer London	11	21	4	17	3
Inner London	3	2	2	13	3

Source: Regular court user interview

When the design of the overall study was explained at participating court bench meetings (see Chapter One), some magistrates expressed concern that the court users' sample was not to include defendants and witnesses, in their view the most important consumers of what lay magistrates do. It was explained that a public survey was also to be conducted and that, if the sample of the public was representative, it would include sizeable numbers of persons who would have attended a magistrates' court as either defendants or witnesses. These 'consumers' are therefore covered in Chapter Five.

Though there are differences in the views of court users attached to each of the ten participating courts, the sample numbers are too small for the differences to be relied upon.

4.2 CONFIDENCE IN THE LAY MAGISTRACY

About one-third of regular court users have a lot or a great deal of confidence in the work of lay magistrates (see Figure 4.2). Only a small minority (8%) have very little or no confidence. Forty-four per cent have some confidence.

Levels of confidence vary, however, according to the type of court user. Court legal advisors and CPS prosecutors have the most confidence (47% and 38% respectively having 'a great deal' or 'a lot' and 2% and 4% respectively having 'little' or 'no' confidence). Other groups exhibit less confidence, but there are important differences between them. The police, for example, are relatively polarised in their views. Whereas 27 per cent have a great deal or a lot of confidence, 19 per cent have little or no confidence.

Figure 4.2

Regular court users' confidence in the work of lay magistrates

	Total	Court clerk	Usher	Police	CPS	Solicitor	Probation officer
Base: All respondents	400	47	35	52	43	115	36
	%	%	%	%	%	%	%
A great deal of confidence	6	15	14	6	5	3	3
A lot of confidence	24	32	20	21	33	22	19
Some confidence	44	34	37	38	40	49	58
Very little confidence	7	2	9	13	2	5	3
No confidence	1	0	0	6	2	1	0
It depends	17	17	20	15	19	19	17

Source: Regular court users' interview
Note: The total figure includes four other groups who were too small to be covered separately.

4.3 CONFIDENCE IN DIFFERENT LAY MAGISTRATES

It is notable that sizeable minorities of all court user groups (between 15% and 20%, 17% overall) say that their confidence in the lay magistracy 'depends' on the individual magistrates involved or the circumstances of the case. Indeed, when this issue is probed 95 per cent of all court users say that there is variation between lay magistrates in the confidence they have in them, albeit nine per cent say that the variation is very little. More than half (53%) say that there is a 'great deal' or 'a lot' of variation, a third (34%) that there is 'some' variation, and nine per cent that there is a little variation. When asked what leads them to have different levels of confidence in some lay magistrates compared to others, perceived inconsistency in decision-making (of which sentencing is the most commonly cited decision), and differences in basic competence with regard to the law and legal procedures, are the factors that most undermine confidence levels (Figure 4.3).

Thirty-two per cent of respondents whose confidence in the lay magistracy varies cite inconsistency or variation in decision-making as the reason. Probation officers and police officers are most likely to cite this factor (49% and 37% respectively) and court legal advisors are the least likely (22%).

Twenty-nine per cent of respondents cite lay magistrates not knowing what they are doing or not understanding procedures as the reason for variations in their confidence in them. Probation officers are most likely to say this (40%), closely followed by CPS personnel and court legal advisors (both 37%). Police officers are least likely to say this (18%).

Figure 4.3

Reasons for varying levels of regular court users' confidence in different lay magistrates

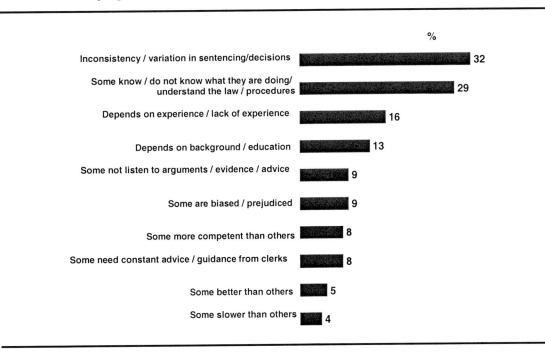

Base: All respondents who have variation in their confidence of lay magistrates (381)
Source: Regular court users' interview

4.4 CONFIDENCE IN STIPENDIARY MAGISTRATES

There is a far higher level of confidence in stipendiary than lay magistrates: 86 per cent of respondents who have observed stipendiary magistrates (compared to 30% for lay magistrates) have a great deal or a lot of confidence in them and fewer than one per cent (compared to 8% for lay magistrates) have very little or no confidence in them (Figure 4.4).

Forty-six per cent of court users who have observed stipendiary magistrates have a great deal of confidence in them, more experienced respondents being the most likely to say this (53% of those who have been in their role for more than five years, compared with 39% of those with 2 to 5 years' experience and 31% of those with less than one year's experience). The court users most likely to express great confidence in stipendiaries are court ushers (68%), court legal advisors (58%), CPS prosecutors (57%) and police officers (51%). Defence lawyers, solicitors and barristers are more muted in their expressions of confidence, but their overall ratings are nonetheless high.

Figure 4.4

Regular court users' confidence in the work of lay and stipendiary magistrates

	Lay magistrates	Stipendiary magistrates
	399	360
	%	%
A great deal of confidence	6	46
A lot of confidence	24	41
Some confidence	44	6
Very little confidence	7	*
No confidence	1	—
It depends	17	6

Base: All respondents who have observed each type of magistrate
Source: Regular court users' interview
* = less than 0.5%
− = 0%

4.5   CONFIDENCE IN DIFFERENT STIPENDIARY MAGISTRATES

Far fewer court users say 'it depends' when asked about their confidence with regard to stipendiary as opposed to lay magistrates (6% compared to 17%). This is also true in courts where several stipendiaries sit and where respondents must be presumed to be able to make comparisons between the performance of individual stipendiary magistrates, though of course in none of the courts is there more than five stipendiary magistrates between which to compare.

This pattern was confirmed when respondents were asked how much variation there is *between* stipendiaries in the confidence they have in them. Only nine per cent of respondents say that their confidence varies a lot compared to 53 per cent when discussing lay magistrates (see Figure 4.5).

In contrast to lay magistrates, the principal factor cited to explain why there is some variation of confidence is the different personalities or styles of different stipendiaries (see Figure 4.6). Twenty-three per cent of court users who said that they had different levels of confidence in different stipendiary magistrates did not offer a reason for their different levels of confidence.

4.6   DIFFERENCES IN THE WAY LAY AND STIPENDIARY MAGISTRATES WORK

As we saw in Chapter Two, the stipendiary magistrates sitting in Urban Court 3 and Metropolitan Court 2 take on the full range of criminal work undertaken by lay magistrates, with the exception of sessions devoted exclusively or largely to fines enforcement and private prosecutions. The clerks to the justices for the four other participating courts with stipendiary magistrates told us that much the same pattern applies in their courts. Respondents were asked whether, setting aside any differences in caseload allocations, the *way* that the two groups of magistrates work is similar or different. Half of the respondents (49%) say that it is quite or very different, approaching one-third (30%) say that it is quite or very similar and the remainder (13%) say that 'it depends'.

Court staff – ushers and legal advisors (43% and 35% respectively) – are most likely to say that the manner in which the two groups work is quite or very similar and solicitors and barristers are most likely to say that it is quite or very different (60% and 57% respectively).

Figure 4.5

Variation in regular court users' levels of confidence in lay and stipendiary magistrates

	Lay magistrates	Stipendiary magistrates
	399	360
Degree of variation in confidence:	%	%
A great deal of variation	25	3
A lot of variation	28	6
Some variation	34	31
Very little variation	9	43
No variation	2	9
Not stated	3	7

Base: All respondents who have observed each type of magistrate

Source: Regular court users' interview

Figure 4.6

Reasons for variation in regular court users' confidence in stipendiary magistrates

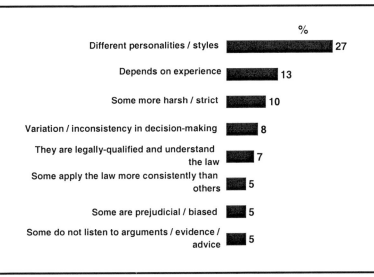

Base: All respondents who have variation in their confidence of stipendiary magistrates (302)

Source: Regular court users' interview

When asked to explain, without prompting, what the differences between the way lay and stipendiary magistrates work are, the most frequently cited answers are as shown in Figure 4.7.

Figure 4.7

Differences in the way regular court users perceive lay and stipendiary magistrates work

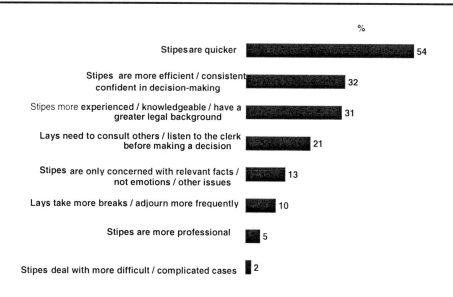

Base: All respondents who perceive that lay and stipendiary magistrates work in a way that is very different, quite different or quite similar (336) Source: Regular court users' interview

Among the 84 per cent of regular court users who think that there are differences in the way lay and stipendiary magistrates undertake their work, stipendiary magistrates are widely perceived to be quicker, more efficient, consistent and confident in decision-making, more experienced and knowledgeable. Defence lawyers and CPS personnel are most likely to say that stipendiaries are quicker at dealing with court business. Lay magistrates are seen to need to consult others and listen to their legal advisors before making decisions. They are also seen to adjourn or take breaks more frequently.

When asked whether these differences hold true for lay magistrates and stipendiary magistrates generally, 57 per cent of respondents say that they do. However, most respondents say that there are greater differences in the way in which lay magistrates work than the way in which different stipendiary magistrates work (37% compared to 10% of respondents respectively) (Figure 4.8).

Figure 4.8

Regular court users' comparisons of the way in which lay and stipendiary magistrates work

	Lay vs. stipendiary magistrates	Different lay magistrates	Different stipendiary magistrates
Base: All respondents	400	400	400
	%	%	%
Very similar	7	11	24
Quite similar	23	38	49
Quite different	32	27	8
Very different	17	10	2
It depends	13	13	6
Not stated	9	2	12

Source: Regular court users' interview

The reasons, unprompted, most frequently given to summarise the perceived differences between lay magistrates are:

- 24%   lack of experience or knowledge
- 18%   speed
- 17%   guidance received from court legal advisor
- 17%   lack of consistency in sentencing
- 16%   personalities
- 10%   some more competent or confident than others
- 6%   extreme variations in strictness/leniency.

The reasons given to summarise the differences between different stipendiary magistrates provided by the much smaller proportion of respondents who think there are differences are:

- 15%   personalities
- 10%   speed
- 7%   some are harsh or rude, others more receptive or pleasant
- 7%   some are more willing to listen to the legal advisor or others in court
- 6%   some more experienced or knowledgeable
- 6%   individual attitudes towards cases
- 5%   more or less consistent.

4.7 RATINGS OF DIFFERENT ASPECTS OF LAY AND STIPENDIARY MAGISTRATES' WORK

A list of different working characteristics was read out to respondents. They were asked whether, in their experience, each characteristic applied more to lay or stipendiary magistrates, or equally to both. The results are as follows (Figure 4.9).

Only four characteristics – use simple language, show concern for distressed victims, show courtesy to defendants and show court courtesy to other court members – were considered to apply more to lay than stipendiary magistrates. However, a large majority of respondents feel that all four characteristics apply to lay and stipendiary magistrates equally.

Fifteen out of the 19 characteristics are considered to apply more to stipendiary than to lay magistrates and, of these, no fewer than seven characteristics are thought by a clear majority of respondents to apply most to stipendiary magistrates as opposed to lay magistrates, or equally to the two groups:

- deal with unruly defendants (61%)
- question CPS personnel appropriately (65%)
- deliver tougher sentences (65%)
- question defence lawyers appropriately (66%)
- give clear reasons for decisions (67%)
- make consistent decisions (75%)
- show command over proceedings (80%).

It should be noted that all but one of the 19 characteristics imply positive ratings, that is, they involve the demonstration of courtesy, understanding, attentiveness, consistency, clarity or whatever the respondent considers to be appropriate behaviour. Only one characteristic is neutrally descriptive, namely, deliver tougher sentences. Though a majority of respondents think that eight out of the 18 normatively loaded characteristics apply equally to lay and stipendiary magistrates, in only four of the 18 do lay magistrates attract more votes than stipendiary magistrates.

Figure 4.9

Regular court users' ratings of lay and stipendiary magistrates' work

		Lay	Stipe	Both equally	Neither
Use simple language	%	19	14	61	3
Show concern for distressed victims	%	19	7	66	3
Show courtesy to defendants	%	17	5	72	2
Show courtesy to other court members	%	16	4	74	2
Ensure defendants understand pronouncements	%	12	25	57	2
Explain decisions so defendants understand	%	10	45	38	4
Require explanation for delay	%	10	45	41	1
Show non-prejudicial attitude	%	9	22	58	6
Address defendant appropriately	%	9	17	70	*
Be attentive in court	%	8	29	60	*
Make appropriate remand decisions	%	7	49	35	3
Deliver tougher sentences	%	6	65	19	2
Deliver appropriate justice	%	5	39	44	4
Give clear reasons for decisions	%	4	67	22	3
Show command over proceedings	%	3	80	13	1
Make consistent decisions	%	3	75	13	4
Question defence lawyers appropriately	%	3	66	25	2
Question CPS appropriately	%	3	65	26	2
Deal with unruly defendants	%	3	61	30	1

Base: All respondents (400)

Source: Regular court users' interview

Note: The percentage not stating an answer has not been shown

* = less than 0.5%

Stipendiaries score better than lay magistrates with regard to 14 of the normative characteristics. Though two-thirds of respondents (65%) think that stipendiaries deliver tougher sentences, it is not clear whether they approve of this.

4.8   COURT USERS' BEHAVIOUR IN FRONT OF LAY AND STIPENDIARY MAGISTRATES

Respondents were asked whether either their preparation for court or their behaviour in court changes according to whether lay or stipendiary magistrates are presiding. Fifty-seven per cent say that their behaviour does change. Solicitors (70%) and CPS personnel (67%) are most likely to say that their behaviour changes, court ushers (23%) and police officers (37%) are least likely to say that it does.

Those respondents who reported that their behaviour changes were asked in what respect it changed. The changes most commonly cited, unprompted, are:

- 32% prepare more thoroughly for stipendiaries
- 22% prepare more thoroughly for lay magistrates
- 14% are more concise or precise with stipendiaries
- 12% stipendiaries understand more about the law
- 10% quicker with stipendiaries
- 5% just different
- 5% more questions from stipendiaries
- 5% more wary about court procedure with stipendiaries.

Different groups of court users report different changes in their behaviour. Solicitors and prosecutors say that they prepare more thoroughly for stipendiaries because stipendiaries know more about the law and ask more challenging questions of them. In support of this, we have shown in Chapter Three that stipendiary magistrates are more likely than lay magistrates to ask questions of the CPS and defence solicitors. Court legal advisors, by contrast, say that they prepare more for lay magistrates because lay magistrates are less likely to know about the law and may need to have it explained to them.

An even higher proportion of respondents say that other court users, as opposed to themselves (73% compared to 57%), prepare for court proceedings, or behave in court, differently according to whether they are appearing before lay or stipendiary magistrates. The differences in others' behaviour most commonly cited are shown in Figure 4.10.

These findings are consistent with what respondents say about their own behaviour and what they say about the differences between the behaviour of lay and stipendiary magistrates. Practitioners say that they prepare better for stipendiary magistrates because stipendiaries know their business better, exercise greater command over court proceedings and ask more questions.

Figure 4.10

Regular court users' perceived differences in the behaviour of other court members, according to whether a lay or stipendiary magistrate is presiding

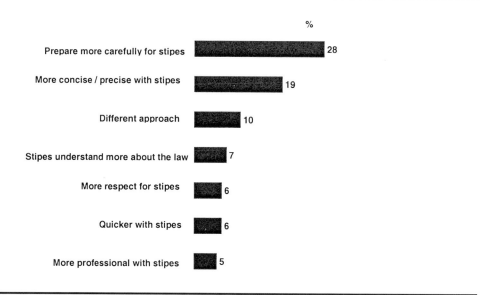

Base: All respondents who think behaviour of other court members changes (300)
Source: Regular court users' interview

4.9 THE IMPLICATIONS FOR THE ROLE OF COURT LEGAL ADVISORS

Seventy per cent of court users say that the type of magistrate presiding in court has major differences for the role of the court legal advisor and 16 per cent perceive there to be minor differences. Only nine per cent of respondents think that this factor makes no real difference to the role of the legal advisor. Whereas court legal advisors are seen to be closely involved with lay magistrates in the work of the court, they are not seen to be nearly so involved with stipendiaries. The data are presented in Figure 4.11.

It is notable, however, that solicitors (84%) and CPS personnel (77%) think that the implications of whether a lay bench or a stipendiary magistrate is presiding are greater for the role of the court legal advisor than do court staff, both court legal advisors (62%) and ushers (49%).

4.10 THE BALANCE BETWEEN LAY AND STIPENDIARY MAGISTRATES

Every interview was terminated with an open-ended invitation to respondents to add whatever comments they wished. Fifty-eight per cent of respondents chose to do so, most of their comments serving to underscore their earlier answers to specific questions: stipendiaries are quicker and more efficient, lay magistrates lack knowledge, and so on. However, 17 per cent of respondents expressed a view about an issue on which they were not asked: they said that there should be more stipendiary magistrates. Police officers (37%) and CPS personnel (27%) were particularly likely to say this, though a significant proportion of all court users (16%) used this opportunity to emphasise that, in their opinion, there is a role for both stipendiary and lay magistrates.

Figure 4.11

Regular courts users' perceived differences in the role of a court legal advisor, depending on whether a lay or stipendiary magistrate is presiding

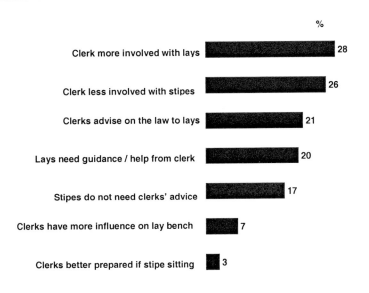

%

Clerk more involved with lays — 28

Clerk less involved with stipes — 26

Clerks advise on the law to lays — 21

Lays need guidance / help from clerk — 20

Stipes do not need clerks' advice — 17

Clerks have more influence on lay bench — 7

Clerks better prepared if stipe sitting — 3

Base: All respondents who think role of clerk / legal advisor changes (344)

Source: Regular court users' interview

4.11 CONCLUSION

Though both lay and stipendiary magistrates score generally well on most of the dimensions on which regular court users were asked to rate them, the stipendiaries get higher ratings and inspire greater confidence. Further, the differences which lead regular court users to say that both they and their colleagues behave differently when appearing before stipendiaries as opposed to lay magistrates are based, as we saw in the preceding chapter, on real distinctions in the performances of magistrates. Stipendiaries do ask more questions and are more challenging. The evidence gathered here supports the statistical evidence of differential decision-making reported in Chapter Three: the appointment of stipendiaries almost certainly restricts to some degree where adjournments are asked for or are granted, and stipendiaries are almost certainly more tough-minded in their sentencing and other decisions.

5 THE COMPOSITION OF MAGISTRATES' COURTS: PUBLIC KNOWLEDGE AND OPINION

5.1 INTRODUCTION

What does the public at large know about who sits in magistrates' courts and how much confidence does it have in them? To the extent that the public is aware of lay and stipendiary magistrates and the differences between them, what does it consider to be the advantages and disadvantages of each group? Since stipendiaries are empowered to sit alone and usually do so, does the public consider that certain types of cases are best dealt with by panels of magistrates as opposed to single magistrates acting alone? Though the 1996 and 1998 sweeps of the British Crime Survey included questions designed to elicit public knowledge about, and attitudes regarding, crime, criminal justice structures and sentencing policy (see Hough and Roberts, 1998; Mattinson and Mirrlees-Black, 2000), there has previously been almost no investigation of public knowledge and opinion regarding specific magistrates' courts' procedural arrangements and functioning. The above are some of the questions that we explore in this chapter.

5.2 METHOD

A sample of 1,753 adults across England and Wales was interviewed in their homes in June 2000. The questionnaire and further details of the methodology employed in collecting, weighting and analysing the data are contained in Appendix B. The data have been analysed by sub-groups such as age, sex, social status, geographical area and ethnicity. When considering some of these breakdowns, regard should be given to the sometimes relatively small samples involved. Some of the differences between groups need to be treated with caution.

5.3 EXPERIENCE OF THE COURT SYSTEM

5.3.1 Contact with Crown or County Courts

Thirty-four per cent of respondents report having attended the Crown Court or a county court as a defendant, witness, juror, observer or in some other capacity. The percentage is highest among those respondents who also report having attended a magistrates' court (65%), those living in Greater London (39%), men (43%) and those aged 45 to 54 (43%).

Those respondents least likely to report having attended the Crown Court or a county court are students (21%), are aged 16 to 24 (22%), live in the North (22%), or report *not* having attended a magistrates' court (22%).

5.3.2 Contact with Magistrates' Courts

Thirty-one per cent of respondents report having attended a magistrates' court. The percentage is highest among men (40%), those living in the South West and East Midlands (40% and 38% respectively), those aged 35 to 44 (38%) and those who completed their education at age 16 (37%).

Respondents least likely to report having attended a magistrates' court live in the North (16%), have not attended the Crown Court or a county court (17%), are students (17%), are persons aged 16 to 24 (19%) and are females (24%).

5.3.3 Respondents' Roles in Magistrates' Court

Respondents reporting having ever attended a magistrates' court were asked in what capacity they attended. Based on the total sample of 1,753 adults, 12 per cent say that they had been a defendant, ten per cent a witness, nine per cent an observer, two per cent a police or probation officer, social worker or other professional and one per cent a licence applicant. Those respondents most likely to have attended as a defendant are aged 25 to 44, male, are in social groups C2 or DE and have finished their full-time education at age 16 (Figure 5.1).

Figure 5.1

Respondents who have been a defendant in a magistrates' court

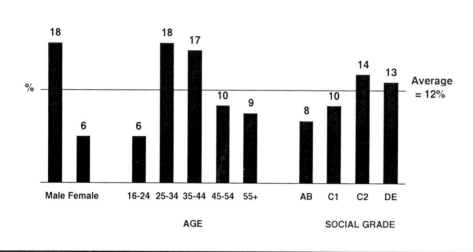

Base: All adults in England and Wales (1,753)

Source: General Public omnibus survey

Respondents reporting having attended a magistrates' court as witnesses are more evenly spread between the sexes and between age and social status groups.

5.3.4 Number of Magistrates' Court Sessions Attended

Two respondents say that they are magistrates. All non-magistrates who say that they had attended a magistrates' court were asked how often they had attended in the previous three years. Almost two-thirds (61%) of those who had attended a magistrates' court at some stage in their lives have not attended in the last three years, a quarter have attended once or twice (24%) and 15 per cent on three or more occasions. These findings suggest, therefore, that approximately seven per cent of the overall sample are fairly or very familiar with magistrates' court proceedings in the sense that they have attended a magistrates' court on more than one occasion during the previous three years.

5.4   CONFIDENCE IN CRIMINAL JUSTICE DECISION-MAKERS

Respondents were asked to say how confident they were that the key decision-makers in the criminal justice system – the police, lawyers, magistrates, judges and juries – are doing their job properly.

Though the variation in confidence levels expressed by respondents about the five groups is not great, respondents are more confident that juries are doing their job properly (68%) than any of the other four groups, lawyers scoring least well (61%). There is greater variation between the groups when it comes to *lack* of confidence. The police attract the greatest proportion of respondents who are not confident that they are doing their job properly (29%) and juries the smallest proportion (18%). Part of the reason for this difference in positive and negative confidence levels lies in the proportions of respondents who either do not know how much confidence they have or say that 'it depends', presumably on the situation or the individual incumbents involved. Few respondents express uncertainty or caution about the police in this regard (fewer than one per cent of respondents say that they do not know and only 4 per cent say that 'it depends') whereas significant proportions (11–15%) of respondents are uncertain or guarded about juries, magistrates, judges and lawyers.

Where respondents feel able to give confidence ratings, they are scored as follows: very confident (4), fairly confident (3), not very confident (2) and not at all confident (1) – in order to calculate relative confidence levels for the different groups. The higher the mean score, the higher the confidence. Juries emerge with the highest score and the police the lowest. All groups emerge with scores at the 'fairly confident' level, however (Figure 5.2).

Though these findings are not directly comparable with those derived from the BCS (the BCS asked different questions about the police, magistrates and judges, did not inquire about juries and lawyers, and did not provide for circumspect 'it depends' replies), there nevertheless appear to be some interesting similarities and differences. Our results indicate the greatest proportion of respondents not having confidence in the police. The BCS found the reverse (only 6% of BCS respondents thought the police did a 'poor' or 'very poor' job compared to 21% and 32% respectively of respondents who were similarly negative about magistrates and judges – see Hough and Roberts, 1998). However, our findings, like those from the BCS, suggest marginally greater public confidence in magistrates than judges, though the difference is not sufficiently large to be relied upon. A higher proportion of our respondents think that magistrates are doing their job properly and more BCS respondents think that magistrates as opposed to judges are 'in touch' (Mattinson and Mirrlees-Black, 2000).

Figure 5.2

Respondents' confidence in various criminal justice bodies to do their job properly

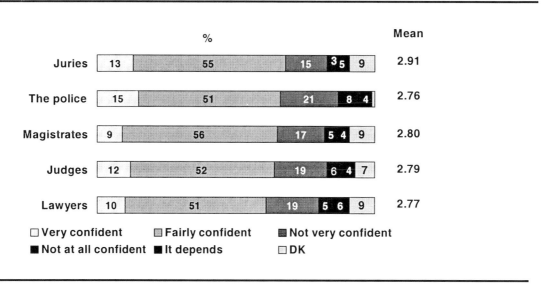

	%	Mean
Juries	13 / 55 / 15 / 3 / 5 / 9	2.91
The police	15 / 51 / 21 / 8 / 4	2.76
Magistrates	9 / 56 / 17 / 5 / 4 / 9	2.80
Judges	12 / 52 / 19 / 6 / 4 / 7	2.79
Lawyers	10 / 51 / 19 / 5 / 6 / 9	2.77

□ Very confident   ▨ Fairly confident   ▩ Not very confident
■ Not at all confident   ■ It depends   □ DK

Base: All adults in England and Wales (1,753)

Source: General Public omnibus survey

5.5 KNOWLEDGE ABOUT THE CRIMINAL JUSTICE AND COURT SYSTEM

5.5.1 Recognition of Key Terms

Respondents were shown a list of terms and asked which they had heard of in connection with the legal system in England and Wales. The terms shown were:

- The Crown Prosecution Service
- Crown Court
- County Court
- Magistrates' Court
- Magistrate
- Lay Magistrate
- Stipendiary Magistrate
- Judge
- Circuit Judge.

The overwhelming majority of respondents say that they have heard of a magistrates' court (95%), the Crown Court (94%), a judge (91%) or a magistrate (90%). However, only a minority say that they have heard of a lay magistrate (41%) or a stipendiary magistrate (37%) (Figure 5.3).

Figure 5.3

Respondents' recognition of key terms in relation to the legal system in England and Wales

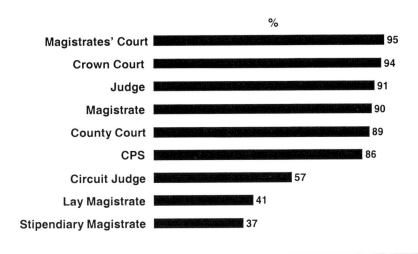

Base: All adults in England and Wales (1,753)

Source: General Public omnibus survey

Men are more likely to say that they have heard of all of the terms shown than women. For example, 46 and 44 per cent of men say that they have heard of the terms lay and stipendiary magistrate respectively, compared with 36 and 31 per cent of women. Knowledge also varies between ethnic groups. White respondents are more likely to say they have heard of all of the terms listed. For example, 96 per cent of white respondents say that they have heard of a magistrates' court, compared with 81 per cent of black respondents and 72 per cent of respondents of Asian origin (though this finding is derived from small samples). Older respondents are also more likely to say that they are knowledgeable. Forty-eight per cent of respondents aged 45 or over and 47 per cent aged 35 to 44 say that they have heard of the term lay magistrate, compared with 32 per cent of respondents aged 25 to 34 and 20 per cent aged 16 to 24.

The higher a respondent's social status the more likely he or she is to report having heard of most of the terms. For example, 53 per cent of AB respondents (for a definition of these groups see Figure A.11 in Appendix A) say that they have heard of the term stipendiary magistrate, compared with 42 per cent of C1, 32 per cent of C2 and 28 per cent of DE respondents. This pattern appears to be linked with educational level. Respondents finishing their education at a later age are more likely to say that they have heard of most of the terms shown than respondents completing their education early.

Respondents who report having attended a court say that they are more aware. For example, 54 per cent of respondents who say that they have attended a magistrates' court also say that they have heard of a lay magistrate, compared with 37 per cent who say that they have not. Awareness also appears to be greater among those respondents who report having attended the Crown Court or county court (54% compared with 37% who have not).

With regard to recognition of any of the terms to do with magistrates' courts (magistrates' court, magistrate, lay magistrate, stipendiary magistrate) almost all respondents (97%) say that they have heard of at least one of them. Only two per cent of respondents say that they have heard of none of the nine terms listed. However, there is a much lower level of knowledge about the distinction between lay and stipendiary magistrates: around two-fifths of persons, and only a bare majority of persons who say that they have attended a magistrates' court, recognise the terms.

5.5.2 The Role of Magistrates' Courts

Two statements were read to respondents; they were asked whether each was true or false.

"Most criminal cases are dealt with in a magistrates' court, rather than the Crown Court."

The statement is true: all criminal cases currently begin life in the magistrates' courts and an estimated 96 per cent are dealt with wholly in the magistrates' courts. More than six out of ten respondents think that the statement is true. However, 20 per cent think that the statement is false and 19 per cent say that they don't know. Men are more likely to give the correct answer than women (70% compared to 52%) as are respondents who report having attended a magistrates' court (70% compared with 58% of those who have not).

"In a magistrates' court a jury decides whether someone is guilty or not."

This statement is untrue: contested cases are decided by juries in the Crown Court, there are no juries in magistrates' court proceedings where magistrates decide issues of fact. Nevertheless over one-quarter of respondents (29%) believe juries determine guilt in magistrates' courts and a further 13 per cent say that they do not know: 58 per cent of respondents give the correct answer. Those sub-groups most likely to think incorrectly that a jury makes decisions in a magistrates' court are young (43% of respondents aged 16 to 24), in social group DE (33%) and those who have not had contact with magistrates' courts (33%).

The later that respondents finish their full-time education, the more likely they are to know that juries do not make decisions in magistrates' courts. A third of those who finished their education under the age of 16 get the answer wrong, compared with a fifth of those who continued their education at age 19 or later.

5.6   THE DEFINING CHARACTERISTICS OF LAY MAGISTRATES

5.6.1 Qualifications

Respondents were asked which of four statements best describe most magistrates (that is, lay magistrates, though this was not said). The results are as follows:

- 33 per cent think that magistrates have a formal qualification in law
- 19 per cent think that magistrates have no formal law qualification but are highly trained
- 32 per cent think that magistrates have no formal qualification but have some training
- six per cent think that magistrates have no formal law qualification and receive no training
- 10 per cent do not know.

It is a moot point as to whether lay magistrates have 'some training' or are 'highly trained': certainly lay magistrates receive more training today than at any time in the past. It follows that just over half of all respondents can be said correctly to identify lay magistrates' principal legal and training characteristic: as not having law qualifications, but as trained. The respondents most likely to know this are: AB (67%); those reporting having attended a magistrates' court (60%) and those completing their education later (66% and 59% respectively for respondents finishing their education when aged 19 to 20 or older) (Figure 5.4).

Figure 5.4

Respondents who think most magistrates have no formal law qualification but have some training/are highly trained

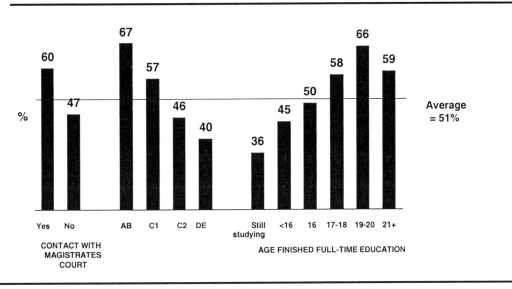

Base: All non-magistrates in England and Wales (1,751)

Source: General public omnibus survey

Respondents most likely to think, incorrectly, that most magistrates have a formal qualification in law are young (55% of those aged 16 to 24), belong to social group C2 (37%) or DE (38%) and report not having attended a magistrates' court (38%).

5.6.2 Sitting Frequency of Lay Magistrates

Respondents are divided when it comes to how often they think most magistrates sit in court (Figure 5.5). Lay magistrates, as we saw in Chapter Two, sit on average almost once a week (for a morning or afternoon), and though minorities of magistrates sit both more and less frequently (at rates which can reasonably be described as anything between once a fortnight or twice a week), some two-thirds of lay magistrates can reasonably be described as sitting once a week.

Just over one-quarter (29%) of our respondents have a reasonable idea as to how often magistrates sit in court:

- 25 per cent of all respondents say that they do not know how often magistrates sit in court
- 11 per cent think that they sit on four days or more per week
- 27 per cent think that they sit two or three days per week
- 19 per cent think that they sit once a week
- 10 per cent think that they sit once per fortnight
- 9 per cent think that they sit once per month.

Of the three-quarters of respondents who express any idea, half think that lay magistrates sit very much more frequently than in fact they do and a quarter think they sit much less frequently than they typically do. These findings are important indications of public perceptions of magistrates' laity and, by implication, the onerousness of the office.

Figure 5.5
How often respondents think magistrates sit in court

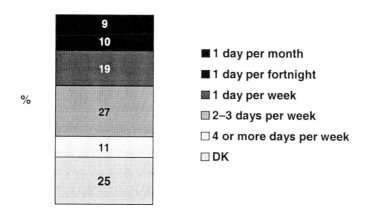

%

■ 1 day per month
■ 1 day per fortnight
▨ 1 day per week
▨ 2–3 days per week
□ 4 or more days per week
□ DK

Base: All non-magistrates in England and Wales (1,751)

Source: General Public omnibus survey

DK = Do not know

Higher social status respondents are more likely to think magistrates sit one day a week (25% of AB, compared with 17% of C1, 20% of C2 and 18% of DE), as are those who report not having attended a magistrates' court. Younger respondents are more likely than older respondents to think that lay magistrates sit in court four or more days a week (17% aged 16 to 24, 16% aged 25 to 34, 10% aged 35 to 44, 8% aged 45 to 54 and 7% aged 55+).

5.6.3 The Size of Magistrate Panels

Three is, by common consent, the ideal and recommended size of a panel of lay magistrates though, as we saw in Chapter Two, significant numbers of court appearances (16 per cent of the court sessions presided over by lay magistrates observed in this study), particularly those for fine default and summary motoring cases, are heard by panels of two lay magistrates. There are also significant differences between courts in this regard: the proportion of sessions presided over by two as opposed to three lay magistrates within the ten participating courts ranged between three and 34 per cent. Furthermore, stipendiary magistrates invariably sit alone and, in Inner London, the majority of appearances are heard by stipendiaries. To this extent it would not be surprising were a sizeable proportion of the public, including those who have attended a magistrates' court, not to know that, nationally, most court appearances are before three lay magistrates.

In fact 39 per cent of all respondents think that three magistrates usually hear a case. Men are again better informed than women in this regard (48% compared to 32%), as are respondents of higher social status (49% of AB, compared to 40% of C1, 37% of C2 and 35% of DE), respondents aged 45 to 54 (52%) and respondents who report having attended a magistrates' court (57% compared to 32% of those who say that they have not).

Twenty-six per cent of respondents think that one magistrate usually hears a case (somewhat surprisingly, the proportion is not significantly higher in Greater London, where a higher proportion of cases is heard by stipendiary magistrates sitting alone, than elsewhere), 11 per cent think that it is two magistrates, five per cent think that it is four or more magistrates and 19 per cent do not know.

5.7   OPINIONS ABOUT THE ROLE AND WORK OF LAY AND STIPENDIARY MAGISTRATES

5.7.1 Awareness of the Two Types of Magistrates

Only a minority of respondents, as we have seen, say that they have heard of 'lay' and 'stipendiary' magistrates, as opposed to magistrates generally (Figure 5.6). We anticipated this result and decided that, in order to be able to explore respondents' views about the appropriate use of lay and stipendiary magistrates, we should explain during the interview the difference between the two groups of magistrates. A brief explanation was therefore read out to respondents as follows:

Most magistrates are called lay magistrates. Lay magistrates are unpaid volunteers who come from the local community, with a variety of backgrounds and occupations. They appear in court about once a week on average, usually forming a panel of three magistrates, and they have the help of a qualified legal advisor.

In addition, some parts of England and Wales have stipendiary magistrates. Stipendiary magistrates are experienced qualified lawyers who work full-time as magistrates and receive a salary. They usually sit alone.

After hearing this explanation, respondents were asked specifically whether they were aware that there are two types of magistrates. Almost three-quarters of respondents (73%) say that they are not aware.

Figure 5.6

Whether respondents are aware of the types of magistrates

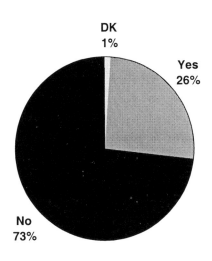

Base: All non-magistrates in England and Wales (1751)

Source: General Public omnibus survey

Certain groups are more likely to say that they are aware of the distinction than others. Those more aware are: of higher social status (39% of AB, compared with 31% of C1, 18% of C2 and 20% of DE); middle aged (37% of those aged 45-54 compared with 13% of those aged 16-24); persons who report having attended a magistrates court (38% compared with 20% who have not); and persons completing their education later (39% who finished their education aged 21+, compared with 28% who finished aged 19-20, 24% aged 16-18, 22% under 16 and 15% who are still studying).

5.7.2 Types of Cases Better Dealt With by a Single Magistrate or Panel of Magistrates

Respondents were asked whether certain types of cases are better suited to be dealt with by a single magistrate or by a panel of magistrates (Figure 5.7). The composition of panels was not elaborated upon. It follows that there is a degree of ambiguity as to whether those respondents favouring panels are giving support to group decision-making or to lay magistrates, though it is most likely the former because, at this stage in the interview, the difference between the two types of magistrates had not been explained.

The results suggest that the more serious the issue being decided the more the public thinks that a panel of magistrates is better suited to decide that issue. Approximately three-quarters of respondents think that panels rather than single magistrates are better suited to decide whether someone should be sent to prison (76% compared to 12%) or the question of guilt in contested cases (74% compared to 11%). Sizeable minorities (12% and 15% respectively), however, think it makes no difference or do not know. By contrast, more than half of all respondents consider that motoring offences (for which the overwhelming majority of defendants are fined) are suitable to be dealt with by a single magistrate (53% compared to 31% who favour a panel) and a further 12 per cent think that it makes no difference.

Figure 5.7

Respondents' views as to who should hear certain types of cases

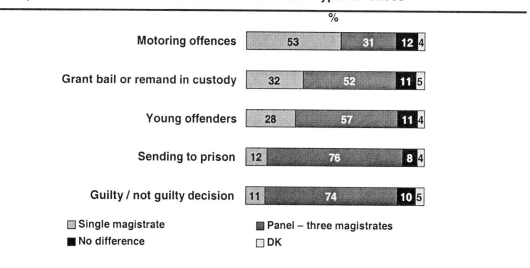

Base: All non-magistrates in England and Wales (1,751)

Source: General Public omnibus survey

Opinion is more divided when it comes to dealing with young offenders or deciding the granting of bail or remanding in custody. Most respondents favour the use of panels for both decisions (57% and 52% respectively) but in each case approaching a third (28% and 32%) consider such cases suitable to be decided by a single magistrate and a further 11 per cent in both cases think that it makes no difference.

Respondents who report having attended a magistrates' court are more likely to think a panel is more suitable for all the decisions than those who say they have not attended (34% compared to 29% for motoring, 58% compared to 50% for bail hearings, 62% compared to 55% for decisions regarding young offenders, 83% compared to 74% for the award of imprisonment and 79% compared to 73% for decisions as to guilt).

5.7.3 Likely Magistrates' Characteristics

Following the brief explanation of the difference between lay and stipendiary magistrates, respondents were asked whether they thought that certain statements applied more to one type of magistrate than the other, or whether there was unlikely to be a difference between them (Figure 5.8). Seven statements, representative of the commonly held views about the relative advantages and disadvantages of having lay as opposed to stipendiary magistrates explored in Chapter One, were put to respondents. The results are as follows.

Figure 5.8

Respondents' perceptions of lay and stipendiary magistrates' characteristics

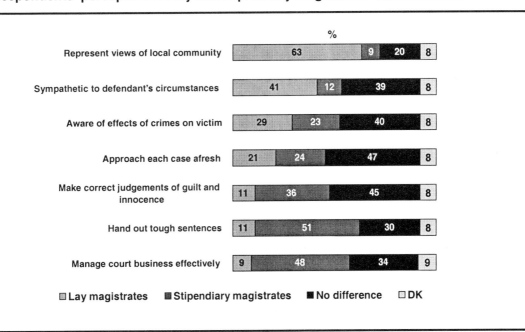

Base: All non-magistrates in England and Wales (1,751)
Source: General Public omnibus survey

The public clearly perceives lay magistrates better at representing the views of local communities than stipendiaries (63% compared to 9%). However, though more respondents also think that lay as opposed to stipendiary magistrates are more likely to be sympathetic to defendants' circumstances on the one hand, and be aware of the effects of crimes on victims on the other, almost as many respondents think that it makes no difference or do not know.

As far as approaching each case afresh is concerned most respondents think that it makes no difference (47%) or do not know (8%). Opinion is almost equally divided as to whether the statement applies best to lay (21%) or stipendiary magistrates (24%).

As for the three other descriptions – making correct judgements of guilt, handing out tough sentences and managing court business effectively – many more respondents think that these apply more to stipendiaries than to lay magistrates, though, once again, sizeable proportions think that it makes no difference or do not know. It should be noted that whereas the first and third of these three statements are normatively loaded and imply approval, the second is purely descriptive: we did not ask those respondents who thought that one type of magistrate handed out tougher sentences, mostly stipendiaries, whether they approved of this alleged characteristic.

Respondents most likely to think that stipendiary magistrates hand out tougher sentences are aged 16 to 24 (59%) and are still studying (63%). There is no significant difference on this question between respondents who report having attended a magistrates' court and those who have not. The latter factor does, however, appear to be linked with the view that stipendiary magistrates manage court business more effectively (55% of respondents who had attended a magistrates' court held this view compared to 45% of those who had not).

Respondents who think that lay magistrates are more likely to represent the views of the local population are in higher social groups (75% of AB, compared with 66% of C1, 59% of C2 and 57% of DE), which may or may not reflect the degree to which respondents feel that the lay magistracy adequately reflects the views of *their* local community.

5.7.4 The Balance between the Contribution of Lay and Stipendiary Magistrates

In conclusion, respondents were shown a list of six statements and asked to pick the one that best matched their view as to who should deal with the work in magistrates' courts. The statements, and the degree of support for them, are set out in Figure 5.9.

Figure 5.9

Who should deal with the work in magistrates' courts?

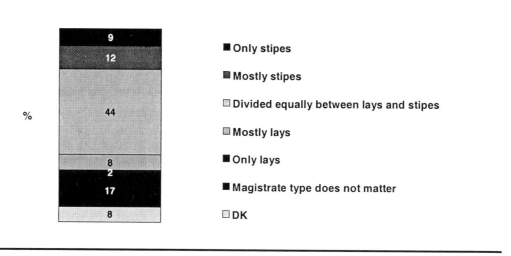

Base: All non-magistrates in England and Wales (1,751)

Source: General Public omnibus survey

80

The majority of respondents think that magistrates' court work should be divided equally between the two types of magistrates (44%), or that the type of magistrate does not matter (17%). Twenty-one per cent think that there should only be stipendiary magistrates, or that most of the work should be carried out by them. Fewer respondents (10%) think the reverse, namely, that there should only be lay magistrates, or that lay magistrates should deal with most of the work.

This latter finding is striking. The overwhelming majority of magistrates' court business is dealt with by lay magistrates, yet only eight per cent of respondents think that this should be the case (although a further 17% thought that magistrate type did not matter). Furthermore, there is little variation across sub-groups when looking at the answers to this question. However, this view is scarcely consistent with the opinion, described above, that panels of magistrates should hear the various classes of more serious cases: were they to do so, lay magistrates would continue exclusively to hear a high proportion of cases or would be members of mixed panels hearing such cases.

5.8 THE RELATIONSHIP BETWEEN EXPERIENCE, KNOWLEDGE AND CONFIDENCE

At various points in the above account it has been established that there is a link between contact with the magistrates' courts and knowledge about the system. In order to explore further how respondents' experience of magistrates' courts relates to their knowledge about and confidence in magistrates and magistrates' courts, all respondents were categorised as having high, medium or low knowledge of the system according to whether they correctly identified the truth or falsehood of all, some or none of the three statements concerning the proportion of criminal cases dealt with in magistrates' courts, the presence of juries in magistrates' courts and the extent of lay magistrates' legal qualifications and/or training. We also focused on respondents who said that they had been a defendant in a magistrates' court, those who said that they had some experience of magistrates' courts but not as a defendant, and respondents who said that they had had no contact with the system.

Knowledgeable respondents according to the above criteria are also more likely to say that they have heard of all the key terms (CPS, Crown Court, county court, and so on) about which they were asked at the beginning of the interview, which is to say that they appear generally to be more knowledgeable. But the differences are greatest with respect to the terms about which most respondents say that they have *not* heard – namely lay and stipendiary magistrates. Whereas the majority of high knowledge respondents say that they have heard of both terms (62% and 57% respectively) only a small minority of low knowledge respondents have (25% and 23%). Respondents who report having been a defendant in a magistrates' court, however, are only marginally more likely to have heard of the two types of magistrates than respondents who say that they have had no contact with the system (45% compared to 35%, and 44% compared to 32% respectively), whereas respondents who say that they have attended a magistrates' court in some other capacity are much more aware (59% and 51%).

Knowledge about the criminal justice system appears marginally to inspire greater confidence in it, but the differences are not great, particularly with regard to the police, judges or lawyers. The greatest difference is with regard to magistrates: 71 per cent of high knowledge respondents say that they are very or fairly confident that magistrates are doing their job properly, compared to 55 per cent of low knowledge respondents. Respondents who report having been defendants in magistrates' courts generally say that they have less confidence in all the criminal justice practitioners than non-defendants, but once again the differences are not great. Fifty-eight per cent of respondent-defendants say that they are very or fairly confident that magistrates are doing their job properly, compared to 68 per cent of respondents who have attended a magistrates' court in some other capacity, and 65 per cent who say that they have had no contact.

Knowledge is significantly related to the question concerning whether panels or single magistrates should make certain types of decisions (Figure 5.10). Respondents with greater knowledge are much more likely to think that panels should decide whether: a defendant is guilty or not guilty; an offender should be sentenced to imprisonment; hear cases involving juveniles; and even deal with motoring offences, though in this regard the proportion of high knowledge respondents who think that a single magistrate is capable of hearing such cases is as large. These are important findings.

Figure 5.10

Respondents' perceptions of the appropriate size of bench to hear specific cases

		Single magistrate		Panel of three magistrates		No difference	
		Total	High knowledge	Total	High knowledge	Total	High knowledge
Bail/remand	%	32	33	52	55	11	11
Guilty/not guilty	%	11	4	74	86	10	9
Sending to prison	%	12	7	76	88	8	4
Motoring and licensing	%	53	43	31	44	12	13
Young offenders	%	28	22	57	68	11	19

Base: All non-magistrates in England and Wales. Total (1,751), High Knowledge (217)

Source: General public omnibus survey

There is, interestingly, no great difference between respondents who say that they have and have not been defendants with regard to the question as to whether panels or single magistrates should deal with different types of cases and decisions.

In only one respect do respondents with greater knowledge about the system appear to differ significantly from less knowledgeable respondents regarding the applicability of different statements (tougher sentencers, manage more effectively, more sympathetic to defendants' personal circumstances, and so on) to one type of magistrate or another. High knowledge respondents are much more likely to say that lay magistrates represent better the views of the local community (76% compared to 51% of low knowledge respondents). Respondents with low knowledge are much more likely to say they do not know in answer to this question (15% compared to 2%).

6 COSTS AND OUTPUTS

6.1 CONTEXT

We are required to investigate the costs of what lay and stipendiary magistrates do and consider the cost benefit implications of altering the balance between them. These are the issues addressed in this chapter. We begin with the costs that fall directly to the Magistrates' Courts Service and move outwards to the costs which do or might fall to other criminal justice agencies. This means that arrangements, particularly for lay magistrates, that initially look inexpensive, take on a more costly hue when wider considerations are encompassed. We could have taken the arguments wider still (by considering the crime preventive cost-effectiveness of different court disposals, for example). Assessments of this kind can be narrow or broad: we have incorporated those elements that seemed proportionate to the questions we were asked to examine.

Before embarking on this exercise a number of general points need first to be made.

6.1.1 The Overall Magistrates' Court Workload

On the basis of information regarding the number of lay and stipendiary magistrates discussed in Chapter Two, combined with the conclusions derived from the observation data reported in Chapter Three, it is possible to arrive at a 'bottom-up' estimate of the overall proportion of magistrates' court business currently handled by lay and stipendiary magistrates (see Figure 6.1).

On the basis of Home Office figures regarding the numbers of persons proceeded against in the magistrates' courts (Home Office, 2000a) and the estimates derived from the most recent LCD estimates of adjournments per case proceeded with (Mahoney 2000), it is possible to cross-check this 'bottom-up' estimate with a 'top-down' calculation of magistrates' court appearances (see Figure 6.2).

The two methods generate similar numbers of appearances, but the conclusions need to be treated with caution. First, different time periods are involved. The bottom-up data are for spring 2000 whereas the Home Office proceedings data are for 1998 and the LCD appearances per case data are for February 2000. Moreover, whereas the bottom-up estimate encompasses all types of appearances (licensing and family court business as well as adult and youth court crime) the top-down data exclude licensing and family court appearances. Hence, we would expect the top-down estimates to be lower than the bottom-up estimates and the proximity of the outcomes inspires a fair degree of confidence.

Figure 6.1

The proportion of appearances heard by lay and stipendiary magistrates

47 London stipendiaries each hear 335 sessions per year	= 15,745 sessions
49 Provincial stipendiaries each hear 368 sessions each year	= 18,032 sessions
146 Acting stipendiaries each hear 60 sessions each year	= 8,760 sessions
Total:	**= 42,537 sessions**
But 27 stipendiaries are dual post-holders, and around 10% of their time is spent in the Crown Court, or on other non-magistrates' court business, reducing this total by 3,377 sessions giving:	
Revised total number of sessions for stipendiaries:	**39,160 sessions**
The average figure of 11.8 appearances per session for stipendiaries gives us an appearance total of:	**= 462,000 appearances for stipendiaries**
As for lay magistrates, there are 30,400 of them (this is an LCD estimate for 2000; the 1999 actual figure was 30,308) and our observation data points to them sitting for an average of 41.4 sessions per year, at an average of 2.83 magistrates per bench, this gives:	
Total number of sessions heard by lay magistrates:	**= 444,721**
With an average of 10.1 appearances per session this gives an annual appearance total of	**4,492,000 appearances for lay magistrates**
Of the **total of 4,954,000 appearances** calculated according to this method, then,	**9% are heard by stipendiaries, 91% by lay magistrates.**

Figure 6.2
Top-down calculations of magistrates' court appearances

Indictable proceedings = 510,000 x average of 3.2 appearances = **1,630,000 appearances**
Summary non-motoring proceedings = 590,000 x average of 1.8 appearances = **1,060,000 appearances**
Summary motoring proceedings = 850,000 x average of 1.9 appearances = **1,615,000 appearances**
TOTAL: 4,305,000 appearances

6.1.2 Magistrates' Court Budgets

A second important contextual factor in any review of costs and outputs is the overall pattern of magistrates' court costs.

The best sources of data on actual costs are the internal MAG/CUREX forms. These are the forms used annually by magistrates' court administrators to claim Revenue Grants from the LCD for every MCC. They are widely regarded as reliable regarding actual expenditure. They are completed by the relevant local authority under ten main and 65 subsidiary headings, and signed-off both by the Chief Financial Officer and an Auditor before being submitted.

Figure 6.3 summarises some of the figures from an illustrative sample of three varied CUREX forms. The figures are useful because they show that the costs on which we focus below – the costs directly attributable to lay magistrates and to premises – are, in practice, relatively small proportions of overall expenditure.

The costs of employing stipendiary magistrates fall outside these figures. Their employment costs are funded centrally. Nevertheless the employment costs of a single stipendiary post – which we estimate as around £90,000 per annum – also represent a relatively low proportion of the total costs of running a MCC.

Figure 6.3

Broad expenditure patterns – a sample of magistrates' courts committees

	Example 1 (£ 000s)	Example 2 (£ 000s)	Example 3 (£ 000s)
Employees	4,885 (73%)	2,269 (68%)	1,423 (68%)
Lay magistrates' qualifying expenditure (travel/ subsistence, loss of earnings, training)	312 (5%)	191 (6%)	40 (2%)
Premises related qualifying expenditure	771 (12%)	547 (16%)	362 (17%)
TOTAL QUALIFYING EXPENDITURE	6,684	3,341	2,085

6.1.3 Workload Ratios: Lay and Stipendiary Magistrates

Individually, full-time stipendiary magistrates inevitably transact much more business than individual (part-time) lay magistrates. Our figures allow us to calculate broad substitution ratios which would apply if blocks of work were to be transferred from lay magistrates to stipendiaries, or vice versa. On average, and using the same figures used in Figures 6.1 and 6.2:

- 1 stipendiary sits for 352 sessions, each hearing 11.8 appearances = 4,154 appearances per annum
- 1 lay magistrate sits for 41.4 sessions, each hearing 10.1 appearances = 418 appearances per annum.

Taking the ratios between these appearance figures means that replacing one stipendiary magistrate would require 30 lay magistrates if they sit three per bench, and 28 lay magistrates if they sit at an average of 2.8 per bench.

6.2 ESTIMATING COSTS AND OUTPUTS

Certain challenges arise when looking in detail at the costs and outputs within magistrates' courts, and the business they transact:

- many of the issues are complex (in particular the crucial issue of comparing like appearances with like). It follows that some of the conclusions are more tentative than one would wish: they invariably come with caveats attached
- much of the management information is less than comprehensive, robust and comparable. This was a surprise, not just to us but to many of the 'insiders' we consulted. The variable quality of several of the magistrates' court service performance indicators and other data sets was not helpful to the research programme and must be an impediment to LCD policy formation
- there is little alternative but to assume that any change in the balance of contribution made by lay and stipendiary magistrates will be at the margins of current arrangements. The largest cost figures (see Figure 6.3) are those for premises and 'overheads' – mainly staffing. Whilst it is possible to allocate these costs to individual courtroom appearances, it is important to realise that these costs will not change in any significant way unless clear operational 'step changes' take place, essentially through closing courtrooms (or opening them) or varying current staffing levels
- several important variables (e.g. rates of adjournments, sentencing patterns) are prone to alter over time whatever change is made to the contribution of lay and stipendiary magistrates. The type of magistrate hearing a particular group of appearances is not the only factor at work influencing some of the issues we need to address.

6.3 SPECIFIC COSTS PER MAGISTRATE

We now turn to calculations of different costs associated with court appearances heard by lay and stipendiary magistrates (See Figure 6.4).

6.3.1 Directly Attributable Costs: Lay Magistrates

Travelling, subsistence, loss of earnings (where they are claimed) and locally-funded training costs can all be identified from the MAG/ CUREX forms. Relevant bench strength figures were also made available by the clerks to the justices for the ten participating courts. We have also estimated what may be appropriate allowances to make for court staff time allocated to in-house training.

From these figures we have calculated the following:

- training, travel/subsistence and claimed loss of earnings: average £429 per magistrate per annum (1998/99 figures: MAG/CUREX data divided by relevant bench strength), or £450 when adjusted to mid-2000
- much training of lay magistrates lies outside the figures given in the MAG/CUREX forms, because it is delivered in-house by clerks to justices and other members of staff. Arrangements do, of course, vary widely, but it has been suggested to us that training activities (including administration, broader discussions with magistrates, etc.) may require between one-quarter and a whole full-time equivalent member of staff at each MCC. Taking a typical figure of half a full-time equivalent of a senior member of staff indicates – with on-costs – a further £20,000 or so should be added to MAG/CUREX-derived training costs. Referring back to the patterns described in Figure 6.3 suggests an additional 10 per cent should be added to the figures quoted above (i.e. a cost per magistrate of £495 per annum)

- taking the average of 41.4 sessions per year for each lay magistrate (see Chapter Three) gives a cost-per-session figure for each magistrate of £11.96
- assuming a bench of three, this gives a cost of £35.90 per bench per session.

These apparently low figures require some comment. Lay magistrates are not paid and their claims even for the sums to which they are entitled (loss of earnings and expenses) are modest (see Chapter Three). Training is typically carried out within home court premises, usually to relatively large groups of magistrates and is usually undertaken by clerks to justices. These arrangements are very cost-effective.

6.3.2 Directly Attributable Costs: Stipendiary Magistrates

The annual employment costs of a stipendiary magistrate are approximately £90,000. There is some variation from area to area in terms of allowances and expenses, but this figure allows for the stipend plus National Insurance and other direct employment costs. From our survey data (see Chapter Two) it seems reasonable to assume that stipendiaries sit in court on 352 half-days per annum (the average figure for metropolitan and provincial stipendiaries taken together, assuming, for present purposes, that all sittings are in magistrates' courts as opposed to other tribunals). This produces a cost-per-session figure of £255.68.

6.3.3 The Impact of Different Rates of Appearances per Session

Standardising the length of session to 150 minutes for both lay and stipendiary magistrates (see Chapter Three, 3.2.2) shows that stipendiary magistrates currently hear 22 per cent more appearances per session than their lay colleagues (12.2 compared to 10.0).

Allocating the directly attributable costs derived above to appearances produces figures of:

- £255.68 divided by 12.20 = £20.96 per appearance for stipendiary magistrates
- £35.90 divided by 10.01 = £3.59 per appearance for lay magistrates.

Though quicker at transacting business, stipendiary magistrates simply cost more to engage than do lay magistrates, at least in terms of these directly attributable costs.

6.3.4 Premises Costs

The clerks to the justices for the ten participating courts, or the chief executives for their MCCs, provided us with a considerable amount of information regarding their court premises and associated costs. The information often included floor plans, internal estimates and a variety of budgetary data. We nevertheless approach the allocation of premises costs with caution. There is considerable variation in how different areas are calculated and allocated to different functions. Arrangements within courthouses vary so much that it is difficult to arrive at typical and thus average figures.

Our best estimate is that approximately 30 per cent of total MCC premises floor space might appropriately be allocated to courtrooms and directly ancillary spaces. The figure to be attributed to lay magistrates (principally assembly areas and retiring rooms) varies more widely, but five per cent might be an appropriate, typical figure. Even where they are in post, the space (essentially office space) occupied by stipendiary magistrates varies greatly: our best estimate is two per cent, but it may be zero in cases where stipendiaries share facilities with other personnel.

If cost data derived from the MAG/CUREX forms, and 'Red Book' data (magistrates' court performance data) on courtroom hours, are brought together then, on the basis of the assumptions above, we estimate an hourly courtroom premises cost of £12.60 (this is derived from 1998/99 figures, but because all involve a high degree of approximation, no adjustment for 2000 seems necessary). Because stipendiary magistrates transact court business more quickly than their lay colleagues (see above), if these costs are allocated on a per-appearance basis, we arrive at:

- £2.58 for stipendiary magistrates' courtroom premises costs
- £3.15 for lay magistrates' courtroom premises costs.

As far as overall space allocated to lay magistrates is concerned, an additional £2.60 per session (or £0.26 per appearance) can be derived from a five per cent allocation of premises costs (using similar arguments to the courtroom figures).

As for the cost of space allocated to stipendiary magistrates, where this applies at all, a figure in the range £5,000–10,000 per annum *might* be appropriate as, in effect, an additional employment cost. On a per-appearance basis, costs of perhaps £1 to £2 might be allocated for stipendiaries, but we are aware of instances where their employment involves no dedicated space.

For all of these premises cost estimates we should stress the heroic nature of a number of the assumptions involved.

6.3.5 Overheads

MAG/CUREX forms summarise expenditure within MCCs in a good deal of detail. If all the directly attributable costs and specific premises costs referred to above are removed, the majority of all costs – in excess of 80 per cent, see Figure 6.3 – remain unallocated. These are largely administrative staff salary costs. If 'Red Book' figures are used to convert these 'overhead' costs in order to calculate costs per courtroom hour then a sum of approximately £180 (range £149–£217) would be appropriate, if indeed it is sensible to make apportionment in this way. Because stipendiary magistrates transact business more speedily than their lay colleagues, an apportionment of these overhead costs on a per-appearance basis indicates figures of around:

- £36.90 for appearances heard by stipendiary magistrates
- £45.00 for appearances heard by lay magistrates.

It *may* be possible to vary these overhead costs in the longer-term. We would stress the point made at the outset, however, that overhead costs will only be shifted appreciably if there are 'step changes' in terms of staffing and premises used.

6.3.6 Central Costs

Costs are incurred centrally with regard to the recruitment of both lay and stipendiary magistrates and for various central monitoring and management functions. We have been able to gather a certain amount of information about the extent of resources drawn on to fulfil these functions but the position is, inevitably, influenced by other factors. Our best estimate is that these central costs are neutral between lay magistrates and stipendiaries and are in any case relatively small in relation to other costs.

We have been given a very thorough analysis of the Judicial Studies Board's (JSB) central training budget covering the training of both stipendiary and lay magistrates through the JSB. Inevitably the position has its complexities: for example, a fee is paid to acting stipendiary magistrates when they attend training events, and a grant is also paid to the Magistrates' Association to support the Association's central training initiatives. An analysis of JSB staff costs for training lay and stipendiary magistrates suggests annual figures of around £193,000 and £59,000 for 2000/2001 respectively; the total JSB allocation for training lay magistrates is around £397,000 and for stipendiary magistrates (both full-time and part-time) around £359,000. Whilst these are clearly substantial sums in total, they amount to about £13 for each lay magistrate and about £1,480 for each stipendiary. Referring back to the costs estimated previously our best estimate is that an additional figure of about 2.9 per cent should be added to lay magistrates' directly attributable costs (representing about £0.10 per appearance), and for stipendiaries an additional figure of 1.6 per cent (representing about £0.34 per appearance) should be added to employment costs to cover JSB training allocations.

Figure 6.4
Summary of attributable costs (per appearance)

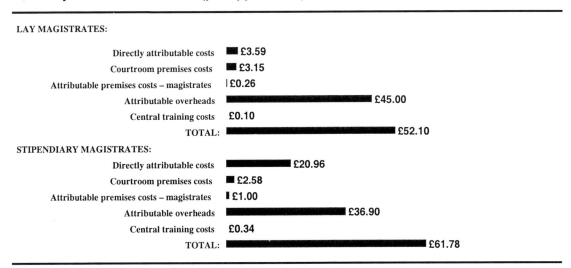

LAY MAGISTRATES:

Directly attributable costs	£3.59
Courtroom premises costs	£3.15
Attributable premises costs – magistrates	£0.26
Attributable overheads	£45.00
Central training costs	£0.10
TOTAL:	£52.10

STIPENDIARY MAGISTRATES:

Directly attributable costs	£20.96
Courtroom premises costs	£2.58
Attributable premises costs – magistrates	£1.00
Attributable overheads	£36.90
Central training costs	£0.34
TOTAL:	£61.78

OPPORTUNITY COSTS

Lay magistrates' time is not a free resource, many have to forego time in their salaried work to fulfil their duties as a magistrate. Some lay magistrates claim back their lost salary, in which case these costs will form part of the direct costs to the criminal justice system (covered elsewhere in this chapter). It is a Treasury convention in assessing costs to take account of both these direct costs, and the costs to society of the donated time. The value of this donated time is measured by the value of the best alternative use to which it could be put – termed the 'opportunity cost'.[1] In the case of employed lay magistrates, an estimate of this is the proportion of their salary which they would have earned in their paid employment for the time they are carrying out their duties as lay magistrates. This is difficult to measure precisely. For instance, the opportunity cost will be lower for those lay magistrates that attend sessions in their spare time (e.g. those with part-time jobs, or those who arrange sessions during their holiday time) or later make up the time they took off. This, though, has to be counterbalanced by the opportunity cost of lost leisure time – also relevant to the 40 per cent who are retired. However, here we have only considered the opportunity costs for those in employment, and suggest an annual opportunity cost of around £3,550 (see table below).

Calculation of opportunity cost

	% of employed magistrates[1]	Salary cost per week[2] £	Annual cost £
Professional/managerial	69	597	
Clerical / non-manual	12	392	
Skilled manual	3	369	
Total [3]			29,100
Total including NI/pension and other costs[4]			35,500
Opportunity cost per employed magistrate [5]			3,550

Notes:
1. From Section 2.2 on magistrates' occupations. 84% of sample gave a current or former occupation.
2. Source: New Earnings Survey, April 2000.
3. Derived from average salary per week, weighted up from 84% to 100%, and multiplied by 52.
4. HM Treasury suggest these amount to 22% of salary costs.
5. Assumes 10% of working time is spent sitting as a lay magistrate: ½ day sitting a week (does not include time spent on training and other bench-related activities).

Effect of including opportunity costs in the cost-comparison

If 60 per cent of this sum (to allow for retired magistrates) is added to the attributable costs, then the average annual cost of a lay magistrate rises from £450 to £2,580. Assuming that each magistrate sits for 41.4 sessions each year, this leads to a revised cost-per-session figure of £62.3 per lay magistrate. Using the same assumptions as discussed in Section 6.3 and assuming three magistrates per panel, this leads to a revised cost-per-appearance in front of lay magistrates of £22.30 (that is, £18.70 opportunity cost to add to the directly attributable cost of £3.59). If allowance is made for the indirect costs of differential overhead and premises allocations, the cost per appearance rises to £70.80 (Figure 6.5).

---

[1] Appraisal and Evaluation in Central Government' (the 'Green Book'), p.17 states: "Most goods and services have alternative uses. Thus, they should be costed at their full value in the next alternative use to which they could be put (i.e. their opportunity cost). Generally current market prices reflect opportunity costs, because households and firms have the best knowledge of their own costs and preferences and a strong incentive to respond to market signals and put resources to their best possible use."

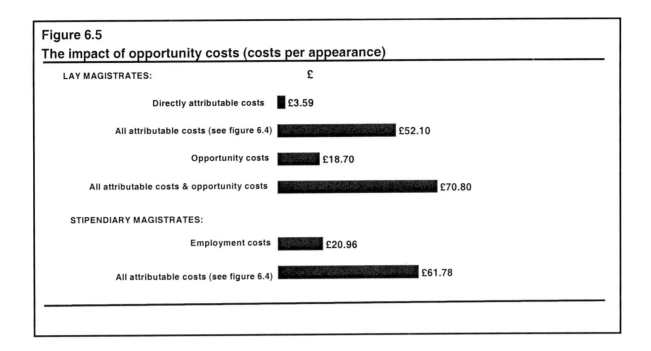

Figure 6.5
The impact of opportunity costs (costs per appearance)

LAY MAGISTRATES: £

Directly attributable costs £3.59

All attributable costs (see figure 6.4) £52.10

Opportunity costs £18.70

All attributable costs & opportunity costs £70.80

STIPENDIARY MAGISTRATES:

Employment costs £20.96

All attributable costs (see figure 6.4) £61.78

6.4 VARYING THE CURRENT BALANCE BETWEEN LAY AND STIPENDIARY MAGISTRATES

Our terms of reference required us to consider 'the financial (and to some extent non-financial) implications of altering the balance between the contributions made by lay and stipendiary magistrates'.

6.4.1 The Cost Implications of Different Magisterial Decision-Making

In this section we review the cost implications from the typically tougher decisions made by stipendiary magistrates as compared to their lay colleagues. To arrive at a standardised way of making comparisons, and to review what would happen if current arrangements were varied, we consider two (totally hypothetical) cases; on the one hand, if current numbers of stipendiaries were doubled (that would provide approximately 200 full-time and 280 part-time stipendiaries) and on the other, the implications of all stipendiary magistrates being replaced by lay magistrates. We should stress that a range of essential assumptions have had to be made in these areas – particularly about current decision-making patterns being retained in the future, and in the different, and entirely hypothetical, contexts we use for illustrative purposes.

6.4.2 Adjournments

The observation data on adjournment decisions by lay and stipendiary magistrates indicate that stipendiaries grant fewer of the requests they receive for adjournments and that fewer requests are made to them.

Figure 3.11 gives our estimate that lay magistrates are likely to adjourn in 52 per cent of appearances for indictable cases, as compared to 45 per cent for stipendiaries. Lay magistrates handle 91 per cent of indictable appearances, stipendiaries about nine per cent. If this nine per cent were doubled by increasing the numbers of stipendiary magistrates in the way we have postulated, the number of adjournments might change as follows.

- Stipendiary magistrates hearing an extra nine per cent of appearances would reduce the numbers of adjournments in this nine per cent from 4.68 per cent (i.e. 9% x 0.52) to 4.05 per cent (i.e. 9% x 0.45) giving a decrease in the number of adjournments of 0.63 per cent.
- We estimate all indictable offences at around 1,630,000 per annum (Figure 6.2). On this basis, a reduction of 0.63 per cent due to the number of stipendiaries being doubled would lead to a reduction of about 10,270 in the total number of appearances (0.63% x 1,630,000).
- This reduction of 10,270 is made up of an increase in the number of appearances heard by stipendiaries of about 146,700 (i.e. moving from about 9% to 18% of all appearances) and so a decrease in the number of appearances of about 156,970 (146,700 + 10,270) heard by lay magistrates.

Reducing the number of cases heard by lay magistrates represents a saving of about £8.18 million, but the extra costs associated with doubling the numbers of appearances heard by stipendiary magistrates (i.e. adding a further 146,700 appearances) represents an increased cost of around £9.06 million, leading to a net increase in costs, according to these figures, of about £0.88 million per annum. This net increase arises simply because the reduced rates of adjournments characteristic of stipendiaries' hearings do not overcome their higher attributable costs.

If all appearances currently heard by stipendiaries were transferred to lay magistrates, similar arguments indicate a reduction in the numbers of appearances heard by stipendiaries of about 146,700 and an increase in appearances heard by lay magistrates of about 156,970. In this case, the reduced attributable costs associated with the smaller number of appearances heard by stipendiaries would be about £9.06 million, and the increased attributable costs of 156,970 appearances heard by lay magistrates would amount to around £8.18 million.

6.4.3 Remands in Custody

We point out in Chapter Three that stipendiaries are about twice as likely to remand in custody when decisions have to be made (37% as compared to 19%, see Figure 3.7). Our data also indicate that, of all remands in custody, 87 per cent are made by lay magistrates, and around 13 per cent by stipendiaries.

According to Criminal Statistics (Home Office, 2000a 15 per cent of all cases remanded by magistrates' courts resulted in custody – on this basis, about 98,000 persons. Using the ratios for lay and stipendiary magistrates above, this would indicate about 12,740 remands in custody arise from decisions made by stipendiaries, and 85,260 by lay magistrates.

We have to insert the caveat that our calculations here involve particularly ambitious assumptions. However, if the numbers of stipendiaries were doubled, it would be reasonable to assume that an increase of around 6,200 remands in custody would be made, assuming present patterns in other areas were retained. This stems from an increase of 12,740 remands through the increase in the number of stipendiaries and a reduction of 6,540 remands from the lower workload placed upon lay magistrates.

To calculate the extra costs of these extra remands, we can compare the current average remand population of 12,520 (see Prison Statistics: Home Office, 2000b, Table 1.1) resulting from an average remand period of 46 days. Comparing this with the average annual cost of imprisonment of about £30,000 points to a cost of one extra remand of about £3,800.

On this basis, a further 6,200 decisions to remand in custody would lead to increased costs (essentially falling on Prison Service) of somewhere around £24 million if the numbers of stipendiaries were doubled. If all appearances currently heard by stipendiaries were transferred to lay magistrates, savings of a similar order might be attainable, on the same assumptions.

We should stress the heroic nature of the assumptions which have had to be made here. However, the figures illustrate two key points: firstly, that stipendiaries are much more likely to remand defendants in custody than are their lay colleagues, and secondly, that remands in custody are very expensive indeed, at least from the standpoint of Prison Service.

6.4.4 Disposals

Our observation data confirm an earlier Home Office finding (see Chapter Three) that stipendiary magistrates sentence more severely than lay magistrates and that lay members of benches with full-time stipendiary appointments tend to sentence more severely than lay magistrates on benches without stipendiary appointments. It is obviously difficult to estimate what the percentage increases and reductions in sentences of particular types would likely be were additional stipendiaries appointed. However, any increase in, for example, the number of sentences of immediate imprisonment by the magistrates' courts would have major cost implications for the criminal justice system as a whole. The Home Office has estimated the costs of different disposals from the Costs and Flows Model (Harries, 1999) as follows (1999 figures).

Figure 6.6

Average unit disposal costs

Disposal category	Unit cost (£)
Fine	(income) – 140
Community Penalty (average)	1,860
Probation Order	2,110
CSO	1,080
Combination Order	4,120
Supervision Order	1,360
Attendance Centre Order	210
Custody (average)	4,930
Young Offender Institution	5,180
Unsuspended sentence	4,850

Carrying out an analysis of the implications of varying the balance between lay and stipendiary magistrates for all of these categories of disposal lies beyond the scope of this study, but we are able to illustrate the general position by reference to the potential implications for custodial sentences (appreciably the most expensive category of disposal) as follows.

We point out in Chapter Three that our observation data show stipendiaries impose custodial sentences in 25 per cent of decisions (for indictable offences) as compared to 12 per cent for lay magistrates. These figures are somewhat higher than those identified by Flood-Page and Mackie (1998) for lay and stipendiary magistrates in the provinces (19% and 11% respectively) but certainly confirm the broad pattern of their findings.

Criminal Statistics 1998 (Table 7.1, p.161) report a total of 30,200 custodial sentences passed by magistrates' courts for indictable cases. Our data suggest that 17.5 per cent of these (5,285) are imposed by stipendiaries and 82.5 per cent (24,915) by lay magistrates. This gives a picture of custodial sentencing under current patterns of:

Lay magistrates	24,915 custodial sentences from 207,625 decisions (12%)
Stipendiary magistrates	5,285 custodial sentences from 21,140 decisions (25%)
Total	30,200 custodial sentences from 228,765 decisions

Effect of doubling the number of stipendiary magistrates

If the numbers of stipendiaries rose 100 per cent to approximately 200 full-time and 280 part-time magistrates, and if current patterns were retained, this would lead to the following sentencing patterns:

Lay magistrates	22,360 custodial sentences from 186,365 decisions (12%)
Stipendiary magistrates	10,600 custodial sentences from 42,400 decisions (25%)
Total	32,960 custodial sentences from 228,765 decisions

The increase of approximately 2,760 custodial sentences (32,960 – 30,200) would, by reference to Figure 6.6, lead to an increased annual cost of about £13.6 million per annum – falling, of course, principally on the Prison Service.

This figure almost certainly overstates the position somewhat. It ignores, in particular, the likelihood that the lower number of custodial sentences imposed by lay magistrates would be replaced by other sentences (in a high proportion of cases likely to be community penalties rather than fines) which have a cost – albeit a lower cost – to the criminal justice system. If we take the average cost of a community penalty (£1,860) then the increased annual cost becomes around £8.5 million.

In very broad terms, an extra 2,760 custodial sentences each year would lead to an increase in the prison population of between 450 and 500 at any time, increasing the current total prison population by about 0.7 per cent.

The effect of replacing stipendiary magistrates by lay magistrates

The converse position is illustrated by considering what might happen if all stipendiary magistrates were replaced by lay magistrates. In this case, our figures indicate that 27,450 custodial sentences would be imposed, a decrease of about 2,750 from the current position leading to an indicative reduction of around £13.6 million per annum, by reference to Figure 6.6, or £8.5 million if we take a community penalty substituting for the custodial sentence.

If the figures quoted by Flood-Page and Mackie for different sentencing patterns (i.e. stipendiaries being only 8% more likely to impose custodial sentences) are more representative of the overall position, cost increases of around £8 million if the numbers of stipendiaries were doubled would be more realistic, again on the basis of the assumptions used here.

6.5 THE COST IMPLICATIONS OF MAGISTRATES' BEHAVIOUR FOR OTHER COURT USERS

If court business is transacted more rapidly (which the evidence shows unequivocally it is when dealt with by stipendiary magistrates), if there are fewer and shorter adjournments, fewer appearances per case and shorter overall completion times, then the costs of other court users (particularly the CPS, defence lawyers, the police and probation staff) will also be reduced. There will be savings to public funds in various guises. This is clearly a vital aspect of the issues which we are asked to consider, but one about which we collected no data (our observers were unable to record the presence in court, for example, of different parties nor follow through cases to their completion) and about which we can make no estimates.

6.6 ADDITIONAL IMPLICATIONS OF VARYING THE BALANCE BETWEEN LAY AND STIPENDIARY MAGISTRATES

The principal potential changes we have addressed are the implications of moving a block of work currently carried out by lay magistrates to stipendiaries, or vice versa. There are, though, a number of other changes we need to consider.

6.6.1 Using Non-Legally Qualified Clerks in Court to Assist Stipendiary Magistrates

It has been put to us from several quarters that there is no reason for (legally-qualified) stipendiary magistrates to continue to have the services in court of legally-qualified clerks: the suggestion is that stipendiaries need no more than an administrator to process documents. Were this view to prevail it would lead to a cost saving per stipendiary of around £12,000 per annum. This converts to a per-appearance saving for stipendiaries of £2.79.

6.6.2 Increasing the Proportion of Business Transacted by Lay Magistrates

We have emphasised how low current direct costs are for supporting lay magistrates, and how low overall costs remain even when making allowances for premises and other costs. We have also emphasised the greater speed with which stipendiaries transact court business. Nevertheless recruiting and supporting more lay magistrates will have cost implications and we believe these are likely to be greater in the future than those we quoted earlier, particularly if attempts are made to make benches more representative (i.e. with higher proportions of younger people, in employment or self-employed).

The current low levels of direct costs arise, in part, because those who currently could make expenses or loss of earnings claims, often do not do so. In our discussion of opportunity costs (above) we point out how much estimated costs rise if an opportunity cost is factored in. Whilst we do not envisage actual costs rising to this level if more 'representative' bench appointments are made as part of notional increases in bench strength, it is reasonable to envisage much higher levels of expense and loss of earnings claims – sums to which lay magistrates are, of course, fully entitled.

If a higher proportion of appearances were heard by lay magistrates, somewhat higher costs could be associated with our estimate of more appearances per case when lay magistrates are involved and because of the somewhat slower rates of progress through the courts (both of these factors would also lead to assumed increased costs for other court users). On the other hand, if current patterns of less severe sentencing on the part of lay magistrates were maintained, average disposal costs would reduce significantly.

6.6.3 Varying the Proportion of Appearances Heard by a Bench of Three Lay Magistrates

Up to this point we have assumed that all appearances heard by lay magistrates come before a bench of three. This is not the case currently (see Chapter Three). There would clearly be savings were the general ideal of three magistrates departed from for full hearings (the recent introduction of early administration hearings (EAHs) already involve either a clerk to the justices or a single magistrate) and if two magistrates made up, as they do to varying degrees at present, *a bench* for a proportion of hearings.

The savings from such measures would not be great. Our estimate of directly attributable costs per lay magistrate per session amount to £11.96. If the proportion of benches with two lay magistrates were 10 or 20 per cent of cases respectively, savings per session would be in the order of £1.20 and £2.40 respectively. That is, there would be cost per appearance savings of around £0.12 and £0.24 respectively.

6.6.4 Increasing the Proportion of Appearances Heard by Stipendiary Magistrates

Were more stipendiaries to be appointed, and the proportion of appearances heard by lay magistrates reduced accordingly, the immediate impact would be to increase the direct costs falling on the Magistrates' Courts Service appreciably. Although stipendiaries are quicker, adjourn less and may well be able to generate savings in a number of other areas, they are appreciably more expensive in terms of their directly attributable costs. Further major cost increases would fall to the penal system were their present more severe sentencing patterns to be maintained.

It is important to stress, however, that the 'base-level' figures estimated above for directly attributable costs are likely to overstate the position somewhat: there are likely to be savings (e.g. to other court users) which we cannot calculate and future costs for replacing lay magistrates may well be greater than current figures (see above).

Further, our figures emphasise the short-term position and change in the number of stipendiaries at the margin. Because stipendiaries transact business more quickly there would in the long-term be opportunities to reduce court premises and their associated staffing costs. On current patterns however, the appointment of additional stipendiary magistrates at the expense of lay magistrates would involve appreciably greater direct costs for both the Magistrates' Courts and particularly for the Prison Service.

6.6.5 Altering the Kinds of Business Transacted by Lay and Stipendiary Magistrates

Up to this point we have assumed that stipendiary magistrates deal with about 22 per cent more appearances in a courtroom session than do, on average, their lay colleagues.

This difference in productivity is of key importance in relation to most of our cost assumptions – because premises and overhead costs in particular have been apportioned on the basis of time taken by individual appearances in court.

The figure of 22 per cent for the greater speed with which business is transacted is an average, however, and for certain kinds of business stipendiaries show even higher differences in their appearances-per-session figures as compared to their lay colleagues.

It is tempting to argue that, if stipendiaries concentrated on the kinds of cases where (relatively) they transact business particularly quickly, cost savings would be considerably greater than those we have indicated so far. To move in this direction would, however, require the caseload allocated to stipendiaries to be even more differentiated from that allocated to lay magistrates than it is already. Because this would, in the short-term at least, almost certainly sour relationships between lay and stipendiary magistrates and because we do not envisage a large-scale reallocation of cases along these lines arising in the foreseeable future, we have made no calculations of the implications of such a policy decision.

6.7   COSTS AND OUTPUTS: A SUMMARY

The key findings from this project which influence the costs associated with appearances before lay and stipendiary magistrates are, clearly, the much greater direct costs of stipendiary magistrates as compared to lay magistrates.

Because stipendiary magistrates transact business appreciably more quickly than their lay colleagues, the gap between direct costs closes appreciably if allowances are made for premises and other overheads, but a gap still remains of somewhere around 12 per cent in favour of lay magistrates even with these additional cost apportionments.

Calculations based only on identifiable financial costs do, inevitably, favour lay magistrates. They make only modest claims for travel, subsistence and lost earnings (much less than they are entitled to) and further support (notably training) is delivered in highly cost-effective ways. Stipendiaries, by contrast, are salaried full-time professionals. Whilst stipendiary magistrates transact business more quickly, there are limits to how much more quickly they can proceed, if only because of the waiting time between cases which is a characteristic of all appearances, whoever hears them.

Other factors which we cannot precisely calculate pull in different directions: on the one hand, because stipendiaries hear more appearances in a session and grant fewer adjournments, there will almost certainly be scope for other court users (police, probation, lawyers, etc) to use their time more efficiently, with consequential resource savings. On the other hand, it is clear that stipendiary magistrates are more likely to impose more severe (and hence appreciably more expensive) sentences than lay magistrates do.

7 LAY INVOLVEMENT IN JUDICIAL DECISION-MAKING IN OTHER JURISDICTIONS

7.1 INTRODUCTION

The purpose of this chapter is to provide a sketch of how the criminal court system in England and Wales compares to other jurisdictions with regard to lay involvement in judicial decision-making. This is a complex question. There is a wide diversity of practice internationally. Because local arrangements are the product of constitutional history, political development and cultural tradition, they cannot sensibly be appraised without a good deal of knowledge about the context within which they operate. For the same reasons institutions and practices are not readily transferable from one jurisdiction to another. We shall therefore limit the discussion in two ways. Firstly, we shall focus on models rather than detailed examples of arrangements for lay involvement in judicial decision-making. Secondly, we shall have little to say about the use of juries, despite the fact that the jury is, self-evidently, a key example of lay involvement. We shall concentrate on near or reasonable equivalents to the lay magistracy in England and Wales. It may be useful to summarise the key characteristics of the magistrates' courts system in England and Wales as we have confirmed them in earlier chapters.

- All criminal cases currently begin life in the magistrates' courts and approximately 96 per cent end there. There is a significant difference between personnel and procedure at summary (lower court) level and indictable (upper court) level, though both levels are heavily weighted towards lay involvement. In the Crown Court matters of fact in disputed cases are decided by jurors; in the magistrates' courts matters of fact, law and sentence are decided, mostly, by lay magistrates.

- Most criminal cases – we estimate 91 per cent – are adjudicated in the magistrates' courts by panels of lay magistrates, that is part-time, non-legally-qualified judges. However, a growing minority of cases (a majority of cases in Inner London) are adjudicated by full-time legally-qualified judges, that is, stipendiary magistrates or district judges as they are now to be known, invariably sitting alone.

- Whether a criminal case is heard in the magistrates' courts by a panel of lay magistrates or a stipendiary magistrate sitting alone is largely an arbitrary matter. It depends on the locality (London has hitherto been distinct from the provinces) and, in the provinces, the vagaries of local history and administrative pressure (whether a stipendiary was ever appointed). Further, in any particular case, it normally depends on who happens to be sitting in court. Apart from particularly sensitive, complex or prolonged cases the allocation of business to one type of magistrate or another is, and current LCD policy implicitly suggests should be, entirely a matter of chance. It does not depend on the nature or the seriousness of the case. Nor do prosecutors or defendants exercise any choice in the matter (though a clerk to one of the ten participating courts informed us that requests to have cases dealt with by a stipendiary are sometimes acceded to).

- Stipendiary magistrates can sit with their lay colleagues, but they rarely do so: it is not the general practice in any class of case.

- Lay magistrates are appointed by the Lord Chancellor, acting in his judicial capacity, on the advice of local advisory committees from a pool of applicants from the public.

7.2   MODELS OF LAY INVOLVEMENT

Doran and Glenn (2000) identify three basic models of adjudication: the *professional*, the *lay* and the *hybrid*. This approach can be further refined by considering whether, in each case, adjudication is done by a single judge or by a panel of judges, and whether different approaches are adopted at the two or more court levels into which all developed criminal court systems are divided. As regards the latter question, it is important to note that resource considerations appear universally to determine that more elaborate (and thus expensive) procedures and the most highly paid personnel are reserved for the most serious offences at risk of the most serious sanctions. However, there is considerable variation as to where the thresholds are set for different criminal court tiers. Thus the proportion of cases dealt with by different tiers varies greatly. This is an important point of comparison. In many jurisdictions the lowest tier of court is staffed by single professional or lay judges. However, it is much less common for a lower tier court *staffed in that way* to deal with offences which are *de facto* imprisonable. In such cases of moderate seriousness, panel decision-making in one form or another, usually in a second tier court out of three or four, is more usual, though not overwhelmingly so.

We know of no jurisdiction other than England and Wales where moderately serious cases are allocated randomly within the same court tier between lay and professional judges, the former sitting as panels and the latter sitting alone. It is true that in some federal and highly decentralised jurisdictions, the United States for example, arrangements vary from locality to locality. This is the equivalent of the diversity of arrangements within the United Kingdom – Scotland and Northern Ireland being different from each other and from England and Wales. What is unique about England and Wales is the way in which, within any one courthouse, the choice between adjudicators may be random.

Finally, there is the question of the appointment of lay judges. This varies greatly. In some Scottish areas and many other jurisdictions (in Sweden and Slovakia, for example) local councils elect or select lay magistrates. In other countries, such as Denmark, a large pool is drawn up according to certain criteria, and then both lay judges and jurors are randomly selected from this pool.

7.3   DEMOCRACY AND LAY PARTICIPATION

In Chapter Two we saw that support for lay involvement in judicial decision-making can be derived from theories of participative democracy. We might expect, therefore, that those countries in which democratic institutions are firmly entrenched are also those in which lay participation in judicial decision-making (either in the form of juries or lay judges) is most developed. It is not so. The jury is a feature of the higher courts in many well established democracies (particularly Common Law jurisdictions such as the United States) but is not employed in many others. This is also the case with the use of lay judges. Lay magistrates or their equivalent are a feature of some democratic jurisdictions, such as Germany and Sweden, but not in other geographically proximate and culturally related countries, such as The Netherlands and Iceland. Many countries within which democratic institutions and ideals are firmly embedded have no lay participation in judicial decision-making whatsoever.

The demise or resurrection of democracy appears sometimes to lead to the introduction of lay participation in an attempt, symbolically or otherwise, to legitimate the criminal court system. The use of lay adjudicators was widely used within the Soviet system, for example, as a means whereby the Soviet authorities sought to demonstrate their alleged democratic credentials. Conversely the jury system is being experimented with in Spain following the reintroduction of democracy in an attempt to enhance the legitimacy of a judicial system historically tainted by dictatorship. There has been extensive discussion in South Africa, yet to lead to legislation, about the introduction of lay 'community courts' for the same reason – the historical association of the judiciary with Apartheid – and there has been legislative and administrative encouragement for professional magistrates to seek the assistance of lay assessors in the magistrates' courts.

However, there are as many examples of lay participation being abandoned for the same reasons. The Irish abolished the institution of the lay magistracy following the establishment of the Republic partly because it connoted British class rule and colonialism. Likewise, several former members of the Soviet bloc – Slovakia and Lithuania, for example – got rid of lay adjudication arrangements on regaining their democratic independence because it was redolent of Soviet-style communism: Latvia is considering doing so. There is no necessary relationship between democracy and lay participation in judicial decision-making: depending on the cultural and political history of the jurisdiction concerned, lay participation can connote either the empowerment of the community (participatory democracy) or totalitarian subjection of the populace (through the rhetoric of 'people's courts').

It should also be noted that the ideal of democracy is capable of being operationalised in different ways in the sphere of the criminal courts. Democracy can be expressed both through the *nature* of adjudicators and their method of *appointment*. In many US states, for example, judges are elected rather than selected.

Finally, there is a need to distinguish between the Common and Civil Law traditions. The former underpins the legal systems of England and Wales, most US states, and most Commonwealth countries. The latter dominates the rest of Europe. Scotland incorporates elements of both. The ideology underlying the Common Law tradition is that law emerges from custom and practice and has evolved in harmony with social, moral and political change. Law is a matter of morality, feel and common sense judgement. Law is a practical art, as is evident from the way in which in England and Wales even professional judges are not trained as judges but as practical lawyers. Societal involvement in the administration of justice is a natural part of this Common Law ideology. The ideology underlying the Civil Law tradition is that of formal rationality. In other words, law is a matter of scientific expertise rather than sentiment. Judges are specifically trained as judges, not as general all-purpose lawyers. In the Civil Law world of scientific expertise there is little or no room for the legally unqualified which is why the involvement of lay persons is often limited to the use of relevant specialist experts as 'lay' assessors.

7.4   LOWER COURT ADJUDICATORY MODELS

It is possible to identify five models for the involvement of different types of judicial decision-makers in the lowest tier or lower tiers of different criminal court systems. We consider each in turn.

7.4.1 Lay Judges Sitting Alone

This model is little used and, where used, is invariably restricted to minor criminal matters. In Scottish towns and cities it is common for district courts (the lowest tier) to be staffed by lay magistrates sitting alone advised, as in England and Wales, by a legally-qualified clerk. The situation is similar in New Zealand for preliminary hearings but not for contested trials or sentencing. In some sparsely populated areas of Australia, lay magistrates also sit alone to deal with minor matters (Skyrme, 1994).

In the US the English lay magistrate model used to be widespread. Over the years, however, the office of Justice of the Peace has become more circumscribed or its functions have been taken over by salaried judges. Paid lay judges (sometimes elected), sitting alone, still exercise criminal (and civil) jurisdiction in many US towns but usually only for offences which are, in practice, non-imprisonable (Abraham, 1993).

7.4.2 Lay Judges Sitting as Panels

This model, the mainstay in England and Wales, is used virtually nowhere else and, where it survives, the jurisdiction of the lay magistrates is generally restricted to minor matters.

Scotland has an extensive lower (district) court jurisdiction comprising lay magistrates, although there are now two stipendiary magistrates in the Glasgow District Court thereby creating in Glasgow the same arbitrary two-model 'system' increasingly characteristic of cities in England and Wales. The Scottish district courts have a far less extensive jurisdiction than the English magistrates' courts however. They deal with substantially less than half of all criminal cases. They do not hear relatively serious cases (that is, the equivalent of English either-way cases) for which English lay magistrates are empowered to impose sentences of imprisonment up to six months: district courts have the power to sentence up to 60 days in prison but in practice rarely impose prison or community sentences. Moreover, they have an overlapping jurisdiction with the second tier courts – the Sheriff's Court summary jurisdiction, in which a legally-qualified judge, a sheriff, presides – the decision as to where the case is allocated being entirely within the discretion of the Procurator Fiscal. It could be argued that the Scottish system of Children's Hearings is a type of lay panel system, but because it also incorporates expertise (including the legal expertise of the Reporter), it is arguably more akin to a *hybrid* system.

Lay magistrates sitting in panels have been retained in many Commonwealth countries, but nowhere is their jurisdiction as extensive as in England and Wales. In New Zealand, for example, the sentencing powers of Justices of the Peace are more akin to those of Scotland than of England and Wales. A system of more fully trained (but non legally-qualified) and remunerated community magistrates who normally sit in panels of two has recently been introduced in New Zealand following the District Court Amendment Act 1998. However, though their jurisdiction is greater than that of the Justices of the Peace, community magistrates are not empowered to try serious offences or to sentence to imprisonment. Further, it is notable that the New Zealand Law Commission objected to the initiative on the grounds that it was undesirable to have legally unqualified persons making decisions affecting citizens' liberty (New Zealand community magistrates can deal with questions of bail or remand and the enforcement of financial penalties).

The New Zealand initiative, which replicates arrangements in other South Pacific states (Western Samoa, Tonga and the Cook Islands), is in part the Government's response to the over-representation of Maori and other ethnic minority members amongst defendants, and the need better to ensure that the New Zealand criminal justice system is sensitised to and representative of a multi-ethnic society (Brookbanks 1998). Arrangements in Australia and Canada vary from state to state but panels of lay magistrates normally deal only with offences that are, in practice, non-imprisonable.

7.4.3 Professional Judges Sitting Alone

This is by far the most widely used model for hearing minor offences. Scotland employs this model in two ways: the stipendiary district court magistrates and the summary jurisdiction of sheriffs (the second of four tiers). Sheriff courts generally deal with more serious cases, as judged by the prosecutor, than do district courts and when dealing with more serious cases still, they sit with a jury as in the Crown Court in England and Wales (the Scottish third tier). In Ireland, both Northern Ireland and the Republic, professional judges sit alone as they do in practically all other Western European countries and most of the Commonwealth.

It is important to note, however, that in many countries the ceiling in terms of case seriousness for the lower courts is considerably lower than in England and Wales. In Denmark, Sweden and Finland, for example, single judges in practice impose no more severe punishments than fines, leaving all cases of any seriousness to the next tier in which a *hybrid* system operates. In Finland, for example, only 25 per cent of criminal cases are determined by judges sitting alone (Godzinsky and Ervasti, 1999). Austria has three tiers: in the lowest a professional sits alone, while in the next (which covers the 'top end' of our magistrates' courts and the low end of our Crown Court) two judges sit with two assessors. Some Civil Law systems – countries as diverse as Turkey, The Netherlands and Iceland – employ no lay people whatsoever at any level.

Many parts of the US and former Commonwealth countries also operate a *de facto* three tier criminal court system. The bottom tier, as we have seen, is often staffed by lay justices of the peace with very limited jurisdiction, while the middle tier is staffed by a lone legally-qualified judge. Although comparisons are difficult to make, the top tier (judge and jury) in most of these jurisdictions probably encompasses a wider range and proportion of cases than are dealt with in the English and Welsh Crown Court.

7.4.4 Professional Judges Sitting in Panels

We know of no criminal court system where panels of professional judges are used in the very lowest tier criminal courts. In some systems with three or four tiers, however, the second tier, comprising legally-qualified judges sitting as a panel, deals with offences broadly equivalent to the top end of our magistrates' courts. Austria is one such case. It is more common, however, for middle tier panel systems to take a hybrid form.

7.4.5 Hybrid Systems: a Professional Judge Sitting with Lay Persons

Hybrid systems – in which lay and professional adjudicators sit in mixed panels – take many forms and many legal systems make use of hybrid arrangements for particular purposes and types of procedure. Thus in the same way that stipendiary magistrates occasionally sit with their lay colleagues in the family or youth court in England and Wales, this arrangement has been institutionalised in the Northern Ireland juvenile court and multi-disciplinary youth panels will soon be dealing with juveniles appearing in court for the first time and pleading guilty in England and Wales. The composition of children's hearings in Scotland is similar. Excepting these specialised areas of work, hybrid models are rare in Common Law systems, although Tasmania appears to make frequent use of a stipendiary magistrate sitting with one or two lay magistrates (Skyrme, 1994).

The hybrid approach, using two or sometimes three lay members alongside a professional judge, is used in many countries; the size of the panel - both the number of legally-qualified judges and lay members – often being related to the seriousness of the case. The model is widely used (Sweden, Finland, France, Leichtenstein, Austria, Slovakia and Macedonia, for example) in middle and upper court tiers, the lowest tier comprising legally-qualified judges sitting alone. The threshold at which cases pass from the lowest tier to the next tier is often far lower than in England and Wales (see, for example, Austria, Sweden and Finland).

In some hybrid systems the lay members are said to be representative in some sense of the community (the German and Scandinavian models, for example) whereas in others lay members are selected for their expertise (the Slovenian and Macedonian juvenile justice systems, for example). South Africa, unusually, has a provision whereby legally-qualified judges have a discretion to call on assessors to sit with them in cases where they consider it appropriate. In South Africa lay assessors can be seen as representatives of the community (particularly in cases where the defendant is from a cultural or ethnic group different to that of the judge) or as specialists with expertise relevant to the case in hand (Seekings and Murray, 1998).

7.5 RELATIONS BETWEEN PROFESSIONAL AND LAY ADJUDICATORS IN HYBRID SYSTEMS

The status and role of lay adjudicators in hybrid systems varies. In some they are the formal equals of the professional judge in every respect. In others they participate only in contested hearings or have no role in matters of law. In yet others their assessment role is solely in relation to oral evidence and they have no access to the written file (see Doran and Glenn, 2000, 42-4). In former Soviet bloc countries which have retained lay participation it is usual for lay members to determine sentence as well as guilt or innocence, and this is an explicit purpose of assessors when they are used in South Africa.

It is often said that, in practice, lay members are dominated by the legally-qualified judges. However, the extent to which lay members are marginalised is difficult to estimate, particularly as no consistent pattern can be discerned from the limited research on the topic. Ivkovic's (1997) summary of research carried out largely in the 1970s in Eastern Europe concluded that the observed effect of lay members on case disposition varied from 1.4 to 40 per cent of all cases. In his own research in Croatia, following the break-up of Yugoslavia, he found lay members to have some but rather little influence. However, Anderson, summarising the findings from earlier studies, argues that lay assessors in Denmark are highly influential and research in Finland has found that though disagreements between lay and professional adjudicators are rarely taken to a vote, nevertheless only one-third of Finnish legally-qualified judges consider lay members to be almost entirely uninfluential (Godzinsky and Ervasti 1999). As Doran and Glenn observe, 'the very presence of the lay members may in itself influence the stance adopted by the professional' (2000, 44).

Finally, little is known about the importance of lay participation in judicial decision-making for the confidence of the public in the criminal courts. In a Finnish public opinion poll nearly half the respondents (44%) considered that the participation of lay members increased their confidence while only 16 per cent thought the reverse. Forty per cent of respondents had no opinion (Godzinsky and Ervasti 1999).

7.6   CONCLUSION

We have not attempted to evaluate the strengths and weaknesses of the different models described above. That would be subject matter for a large scale research project in its own right. Moreover, the value of such an exercise would be questionable. The adoption of one adjudication arrangement as against another is so much a part of historical development and cultural tradition that any evaluation would be difficult to conduct and the lessons would be unlikely to be straightforwardly translatable. What is acceptable and works well in one environment may not in another. An important element in the delivery of any criminal justice system is public confidence. A populace steeped in one cultural tradition may not have confidence in the arrangements favoured by those of a different cultural tradition. In Britain, as we noted in Chapter Two, the participation of unpaid lay volunteers in the delivery of public services is an important and deeply-rooted aspect of civic culture. It is not so to the same degree elsewhere.

This chapter has nevertheless demonstrated two important lessons. Firstly, there is a bewildering variety of models for judicial decision-making in use worldwide in the lower courts. Almost any model can be justified on one criterion or another, but whether any one model would command public confidence in every jurisdiction is another matter entirely. Secondly, the heavy dependence on lay judges in England and Wales appears to be unique. In no other jurisdiction of which we are aware is such a high proportion of criminal cases, including cases of medium seriousness attracting serious penalties, heard by lay persons. Moreover, it is notable that almost all Common Law systems which used to rely heavily on a variant of the English and Welsh system of lay magistrates have substantially abandoned it in favour of professional judges.

8   CONCLUSIONS & DISCUSSION

8.1   INTRODUCTION

In this concluding chapter we summarise the main findings in relation to the principal issues we were commissioned to investigate. We also set out some of the implications of those findings for the debate about the future composition of the magistrates' courts. We make no recommendations as to what balance there should be between the contribution of lay and stipendiary magistrates to the work of the magistrates' courts: we do not consider it our place to do so, not least because this report does not cover in depth all the considerations which need to be taken into account

We make suggestions, however, on how the debate regarding the future composition of the magistracy might in future be better informed. We do so because, during the course of our research, we have uncovered a number of defects in the way information is currently collected and recorded within the Magistrates' Courts Service. These defects we count among our findings. If our suggestions are acted on it should mean that:

- there is less need to commission research of the type reported here
- the work of magistrates should be less prey to stereotypical portrayals
- much of the information we have assembled should routinely be available to those who manage the system. That way public debate and policy formation will better be evidence based.

8.2   THE COMPOSITION OF THE MAGISTRACY AND THE AMOUNT AND TYPE OF WORK DONE BY THE MEMBERSHIP

8.2.1 Lay Magistrates

Because lay magistrates are part-time volunteers they exercise a wider margin of appreciation than do salaried professionals as to how much work they are able and willing to do. The overwhelming majority of lay magistrates give a great deal more of their time to their office than the minimum they are advised they should be able and prepared to give:

- they sit in court for an average of 41.4 occasions per annum
- when travelling time, assembly beforehand and debriefing afterwards is taken into account, this typically means a full half day roughly once a week if annual and bank holidays are taken into account.

In addition, for all magistrates, but in particular for those who are elected by their peers to bench offices, there is the time spent attending training sessions (an increasingly onerous undertaking given the mass of legislative and procedural change of recent years), administrative and liaison committee meetings, and so on. Most lay magistrates devote the equivalent of more than a full working week to such activities during the course of a year and senior magistrates give far more time, albeit much of it in what would otherwise be their free time, during evenings and weekends.

This substantial time commitment has implications for the sort of people who become magistrates. Though the lay magistracy is now gender balanced and has made great strides towards ethnic representativeness, magistrates are drawn overwhelmingly (four-fifths of them) from the ranks of management and the professions. Two-fifths of them have retired from full-time work. Of those in work, fewer than a quarter claim loss of earnings and a significant minority do not even claim their allowable expenses. This does not necessarily reflect their affluence: many magistrates' employers continue to pay them while they are undertaking their public duties and many live sufficiently close to their duties not to incur significant expenses. This research suggests that, nevertheless, the personal circumstances of many lay magistrates is clearly such that they do not need to worry about the financial implications of the office. In this respect the lay magistrate body cannot be considered representative of the community at large.

If the profile of the lay magistracy leans towards those who have retired from work, this is even more true of sitting patterns: older, longer service magistrates sit more frequently than their younger, shorter service colleagues. They are also able and willing to give even more time than are their younger employed colleagues. Younger magistrates comment that, while they would like to sit more frequently, they cannot afford the time.

There is no consensus among existing magistrates as to the value of their each undertaking a more or less equal number of sittings: the arguments for flexibility and bench equality of contribution are fairly evenly balanced. But it would almost certainly disturb the broadly non-hierarchical ethos of most benches were there to be substantially greater inequality than there already is in the contribution members make to the work of the court.

This means that the direction of future policy will be dictated by the importance attached to keeping within limits the frequency with which lay magistrates sit in court and maximising its representativeness in terms of age and social class. A more socially representative magistracy could almost certainly be recruited, but:

- the members would be unlikely to be so willing or able to sit as often as many lay magistrates do today
- we believe that more socially representative recruits would be more likely to claim loss of earnings and expenses.

Which is to say that a more socially representative lay magistracy would be a more expensive one in terms of the direct costs falling to the Magistrates' Courts Service.

Finally, it is surprising that many benches, and the LCD centrally (though there are plans afoot to remedy this), currently are unable to make available accurate up-to-date information about the social composition of the lay magistracy. If the lay magistracy is to be a convincing exemplar of participatory democracy and the 'active community' it seems reasonable that there should be greater transparency about who dispenses justice in the name of the community. It should not be difficult to make available publicly up-to-date statistics as to the age, ethnic identity, employment status and normal occupation of the full bench as opposed to new recruits. Not to do so invites the damaging suggestion, made by many critical commentators over the years, that the lay magistracy is a secretive self-propagating elite.

8.2.2 Stipendiary Magistrates

Stipendiary magistrates, now called district judges, are salaried, legally-qualified, professional judges who work according to a contract. They are paid approximately £90,000 per annum when on-costs are taken into account. However, there seems to be some uncertainty within the LCD as to what this does and should mean in terms of the amount of time spent in court and there is certainly variation between individuals as to the amount of time that is spent in court, over and above other judicial duties on which individuals may be employed.

There is also some uncertainty, wryly pointed to by some justices' clerks, as to the line of management accountability for the performance of stipendiary magistrates – whether it lies locally to the chief executive and the MCC, or centrally to the LCD. This uncertainty is perhaps reflected in the fact that hitherto no single agent has been given responsibility for recording precisely how often individual stipendiaries do sit in court, whether it be in the Crown Court or the magistrates' court (for dual post-holders), whether at home (the court to which they are normally attached) or away (other courts, when occasionally assisting them).

These ambiguities and uncertainties will no doubt be resolved now that all stipendiary magistrates have been brought into a single national service under a Senior District Judge. Suffice it to say that stipendiaries currently sit in court more frequently in the provinces than in London, but in both locations their contribution to court work is closer to four than five days a week during a 44-week working year.

8.2.3 The Allocation of Court Work Between Lay and Stipendiary Magistrates

In the same way that stipendiaries assist courts other than those to which they regularly are attached in order to deal with complex, lengthy or sensitive proceedings, so they tend to be allocated the more complex court business at home. This fact prompts the perception among lay magistrates in courts without full-time stipendiaries that the appointment of a stipendiary will mean the lay magistrates being deprived of more interesting and challenging work. Further, it suggests to many lay magistrates that a decision to increase the number of stipendiaries nationally likely signals the progressive marginalisation of lay magistrates, reducing them to handling routine minor summary offences – work that they do of course currently undertake, but are unwilling to offer so much of their voluntary unpaid time exclusively to hear.

The idea that the appointment of a stipendiary will lead lay magistrates to become second class magistrates is not the official view. Stipendiaries, the LCD emphasises, are expected to undertake the full range of magistrates' court business. Yet, self-evidently, stipendiaries are not merely full-time judges: they are legally-qualified professionals. It scarcely makes sense for the well-rewarded skills of stipendiaries not to be employed on court business which will benefit most from the application of those skills. The LCD view is that lay and stipendiary magistrates complement each other: this consideration informs decisions to appoint stipendiaries. Yet, as everyone familiar with the operation of the magistrates' courts is aware, the appointment of additional stipendiary magistrates is a sensitive issue as is the relationship between new appointees and their lay colleagues. Relationships between longstanding stipendiary appointees and their lay colleagues are generally harmonious, but the doctrine of complementarity is believed by many lay magistrates to be rhetorical for the long-term.

The evidence gathered in this study suggests that stipendiaries do not deal with the same sort of business as lay magistrates. Their allocation of cases tends towards the 'heavy'. That is, though they certainly deal with summary matters, most of their sittings involve a mixed complement of either-way criminal cases. Seldom do they take courts to which large batches of summary motoring cases are allocated, or specialist fines enforcement or private prosecutions for the non-payment of television licences, and the like. There is no common pattern to the allocation of business between lay and stipendiary magistrates, however. In some courts, clerks to justices design lists specifically for their stipendiaries, typically loading them with more cases than they consider a panel of lay magistrates could handle in an equivalent time. In other courts stipendiaries are merely allocated one of the generally drawn-up lists, and are expected to help out their lay colleagues if, as anticipated, they complete their list before the end of the session. The allocational strategy adopted by clerks depends on the personalities of the magistrates involved and the historical relationships between the lay and stipendiary colleagues within the bench. At present, however, there is little evidence that the appointment of stipendiaries has seriously deprived their lay colleagues of dealing with challenging cases.

In one respect, however, there is an almost universal practice. Stipendiary magistrates invariably sit alone. They very seldom chair mixed panels comprising lay colleagues. It is occasionally done to give a new magistrate an interesting training experience. In a few courts it is sometimes done in the family or youth court. However, the view seems generally to prevail that to put lay and stipendiary magistrates together is a waste of resources.

8.3   THE ALLOCATION OF CASES IN THE LIGHT OF PRACTICE IN OTHER JURISDICTIONS

The fact that lay and stipendiary magistrates almost always sit separately, the former in panels and the latter alone, might be considered partly to give the lie to the doctrine of complementarity. It suggests that lay and stipendiary magistrates have nothing to learn from each other or to contribute jointly to decisions. It highlights three observations which emerge from our consideration of the involvement of lay persons in judicial decision-making in other jurisdictions.

- Whereas different criminal court systems employ *either* lay *or* professional judges in the lowest tier of courts, in no other jurisdiction of which we are aware is it a matter of pure chance, rather than a matter of policy, whether a defendant is dealt with by one type of judge or another.
- Though many Common Law jurisdictions employ lay magistrates to deal with summary matters for which the outcome is typically a financial or other community-based penalty, in no other jurisdiction of which we are aware do lay judges alone or in panels deal with offences of the seriousness dealt with in the English and Welsh magistrates' courts by lay magistrates.
- Though the functional equivalent of lay magistrates are employed in many Civil Law criminal justice systems, they generally sit alongside professional judges on moderately serious cases for which the penalty is liable to be imprisonment, or where the case is contested.

What is unusual, and arguably odd, about the English and Welsh system, is that straightforward minor matters in which a plea of guilty has been entered are usually dealt with by panels of magistrates, and serious contested matters are increasingly liable to be decided – both the question of guilt and sentence – by a single magistrate. This feature of our system crosses few people's minds until, with either the actuality or the prospect of additional stipendiary magistrate appointments, combined with government proposals that defendants' access to trial by jury be curtailed, what has previously been a technical possibility, becomes a likely outcome. We return to this issue.

8.4 THE QUALITY OF MAGISTRATES' WORK AND HOW THEY ARE SEEN

8.4.1 Regular Observers' Perceptions

Lay magistrates have for some time appraised each other's performance. We asked our court observers to apply much the same criteria as the magistrates apply to each other. The results were almost entirely positive. Our observers found both lay and stipendiary magistrates to be overwhelmingly attentive, to demonstrate a non-prejudicial attitude and to address defendants and other parties with courtesy.

On other dimensions, however, though most lay magistrates score positively, a minority do not, whereas stipendiaries again score almost uniformly well. A minority of lay magistrates, which inevitably means chairmen acting as spokespersons for their lay colleagues, do not exhibit those qualities which almost certainly develop from confidence in the job. That is:

- they do not always show command over the proceedings
- they do not always require explanations from those court participants who cause delay.

This finding is confirmed by other sources. Our survey of regular court users (solicitors, CPS personnel, probation officers, and so on) reveals that there is greater confidence in stipendiaries than lay magistrates, in part because the performance of different lay magistrates is said to vary. Lay magistrates are perceived to be more inconsistent in their decisions: such variation reduces confidence in the lay magistracy as a whole. Further, many regular court users say that the way lay and stipendiary magistrates work is different. Stipendiary magistrates are widely perceived to be more efficient in dealing with court business, which means that they are quicker, more consistent and confident in their decision-making.

These perceived differences lead certain court practitioners to say that they behave differently, and they think that their colleagues behave differently, when appearing before one type of magistrate compared to another. Solicitors and CPS personnel say that they prepare more thoroughly for stipendiaries and take care to be more concise or precise when making applications to them. They do so because they are more liable to be challenged from the bench. Court legal advisors, by contrast, tend to say that they prepare more thoroughly for lay magistrates because the magistrates are more likely to need advice.

8.4.2 Differences in Magistrates' Performance

The perceived differences in the way lay and stipendiary magistrates work is mirrored in the actual differences in performance which our large sample of court observations in ten different courts revealed.

Stipendiaries are everywhere quicker at dealing with all categories of court business. This is partly because of the obvious consideration that in most cases they need to consult neither colleagues nor the court legal advisor. They sit alone and they possess legal expertise. They very seldom retire, and when they do retire it is for periods so short as to suggest that the purpose is not to consult legal texts.

However, the greater dispatch with which stipendiaries deal with cases is not attributable just to the fact that they stay in court. They are quicker at making decisions anyway. This is not because they are less inquisitorial. On the contrary, the reason why solicitors and CPS personnel say they

111

prepare better for appearances before stipendiaries is that they *are* liable to be asked more questions. Our court observations show unequivocally that hearings before stipendiaries involve more questions being asked of all parties and at all stages than at hearings before lay magistrates. Furthermore, whereas the fewer questions at hearings before lay magistrates are almost as liable to come from the court legal advisor as from the bench, stipendiary magistrates invariably ask questions and explain decisions themselves.

The greater speed of stipendiary magistrates is naturally mostly in relation to matters requiring greater consideration: that is, decisions about which lay magistrates are likely to need to consult their legal advisor and each other. However, the greater speed with which stipendiaries dispatch individual appearances is not converted into an equivalent enhanced efficiency when it comes to appearances dealt with per court session. The reason for this is that during most court sessions where defendants are present, there is inevitable delay between court appearances. This impediment is unlikely to diminish given the emphasis now placed on court users not having to wait unduly for their case to come on and the wider use of structured court appearance time-tabling. There is less delay between appearances before stipendiaries than lay magistrates, but the difference is not great. These delays, many of which are inevitable (waiting for the defendant to come from the assembly area, getting documents signed, and so on) act as a brake on the greater efficiency of stipendiaries.

The greater the number of appearances dealt with per court session, the greater is the overall proportion of the session taken up by delays between appearances. Thus whereas stipendiary magistrates dispatch some categories of appearances much faster than lay magistrates – overall they process only 22 per cent more appearances during standardised sessions of two and a half hours. Though the efficiency gain would almost certainly be greater were stipendiaries to deal with exactly comparable caseloads to lay magistrates – we estimate that stipendiaries would deal with approximately 30 per cent more like-for-like appearances. This is, nevertheless a more modest gain than some previous commentators have estimated (see, for example, Seago et al., 1995, 68 and 115).

8.5 THE DECISION-MAKING OF LAY AND STIPENDIARY MAGISTRATES

The fact that stipendiaries deal more expeditiously with court work, assuming that they meet or better achieve all the due process standards of justice which one might wish to apply, is not of course the only consideration when assessing whether or not to increase their number. There are the implications of any differences in the pattern of decisions they make. These may impact on both costs and the legitimacy of stipendiaries with the public at large.

Successive studies have found significant differences in the decision-making patterns of different benches of lay magistrates (see Chapter One) and one Home Office study (Flood-Page and Mackie 1998, Chapter Seven) has found that stipendiaries tend to sentence more severely than their lay colleagues. The question therefore arises as to whether there are other differences in the decision-making of lay and stipendiary magistrates and whether the appointment of full-time stipendiaries has an impact on the local lay judicial culture or whether stipendiaries embody a judicial culture in their own right.

The findings from this study are less conclusive regarding this question than we would have wished. This is partly because the Magistrates' Courts Service does not have the data recording system that any large scale public service needs for effective management. There are three incompatible relatively antiquated computer systems in use in different magistrates' courts and most of these systems have been adapted locally so that no common coding system can be employed easily to transfer court register data electronically for central analysis beyond the compilation of the criminal statistics. Further, the court register information that is stored on computer locally does not include details that enable one routinely to establish how efficiently cases are being processed. The time that cases take in court is not recorded, nor in most courts the name or type of magistrate who chaired the bench. Moreover, appearances are not linked electronically so that the LCD is forced, three times annually, to undertake surveys to establish how often cases are being adjourned and how long they take to deal with from first listing to completion (see Mahoney, 2000).

Thus the sort of large scale analysis of court register data that we planned to undertake in the event proved neither possible within the time and resources available nor was the work that we were able to accomplish as useful as it might have been. We were ultimately able to analyse the court registers for only three courts – two within the observation sample and one without. This enabled us to do little more than establish the allocation of types of cases between stipendiary and lay magistrates in two courts, a pattern which may not be representative. Moreover, despite concentrating our major data collection effort on the observation of triable-either-way criminal cases, variations in the pattern of decision-making between courts, and the small numbers of offences of particular types dealt with by stipendiary and lay magistrates in individual courts, has meant that it is not possible to apply more rigorous statistical techniques so that we can be certain that the decisions being considered involve like cases. It follows that several of our conclusions are less robust than we would wish.

We begin with sentencing, the decisions about which we are most confident. Our data confirm Flood-Page and Mackie's earlier finding that stipendiaries impose more severe penalties than their lay colleagues. They impose immediate custodial penalties more often and financial penalties and conditional discharges less often. The difference is consistent across all the courts with stipendiaries in the study. Our data also confirm Flood-Page and Mackie's other finding, namely, that lay magistrates on benches with stipendiaries sentence more severely than on benches without. There appears to be an acculturation effect.

Given their pattern of sentencing we hypothesised that stipendiaries would also make greater proportionate use of remands in custody. The data across all ten courts suggest that this is the case. However, the overall difference is attributable to the greater use of custodial remands by the stipendiaries in two out of the six courts with stipendiaries. Elsewhere there is no apparent difference. The data nevertheless suggest that were the overall number of stipendiary appointments to be increased then, other things being equal, the size of the pre-trial prison population would be increased.

While greater reliance on the use of custody increases the direct costs falling to the criminal justice system, any tendency of stipendiaries more often to resist applications for adjournments would save appearances and the costs falling to both the courts and other agencies. We hypothesised that the observed tendency of stipendiaries more often to challenge applications from both the defence and prosecution would have this outcome both directly (refusals) and indirectly (fewer applications being made to them). Both hypotheses are substantiated. There is a general tendency for fewer applications to adjourn to be agreed to by stipendiaries compared to lay magistrates and it appears that proportionately fewer applications to adjourn are made to stipendiaries.

The data also show that adjournments both applied for to stipendiaries and granted by them are for marginally shorter periods than is the case before lay magistrates.

As far as trials and findings of guilt are concerned, too few of the trials that were observed were completed for us to come to any conclusion as to whether there is a difference between lay and stipendiary magistrates. The so-called case-hardening hypothesis (see Chapter One) is therefore untested. As far as the committal rate to the Crown Court is concerned, there is no apparent difference between the two types of magistrate.

8.6   THE COST IMPLICATIONS OF USING LAY AND STIPENDIARY MAGISTRATES

Most commentators have always assumed that, setting aside all other arguments about the merits of having a lay magistracy compared to professional judges, lay magistrates have the supreme merit that they are cheap. They are unpaid volunteers, though able to claim expenses and modest loss of earnings. Our conclusion on costs, as is so often the case, is that it depends on the factors included in the calculations.

A simple analysis of the direct costs for the Magistrates' Courts Service of using the two types of magistrates shows, not surprisingly, that lay magistrates are extraordinarily cheap compared to stipendiaries. The direct average cost of a lay justice we calculate at £495 per annum, that of a stipendiary £90,000. When these baseline direct costs are attached to the different elements which determine the productivity of the two groups – whether the magistrates sit alone or in panels, the number of court sessions attended and the relative throughput of cases during those sessions – they convert to £3.59 per appearance for lay magistrates and £20.96 for stipendiaries.

When all the overheads are brought into the equation (premises, administrative support staff, and so on) the cost per appearance for lay and stipendiary magistrates becomes £52.10 and £61.78 respectively.

This is a superficial view of costs, however. There is first the question as to whether stipendiary magistrates need to have allocated to them, as is at present the case, a legally-qualified court legal advisor. It has been suggested to us that this arrangement represents an indefensible, unnecessary luxury. Stipendiaries are legally-qualified. It may be reassuring that they have in front of them a second legal opinion on which they can call but it is not a requisite. Were this view to prevail then the cost of any additional stipendiary would be offset by the saving of one legally-qualified member of the Magistrates' Court Service and the employment instead of a court administrator. We assess this saving at £12,000 per annum.

A further consideration concerns the extent to which any change in the contribution made by lay and stipendiary magistrates is contemplated. We assume, because the Lord Chancellor has said so, that the Government 'is committed to the principle of the lay magistracy continuing to play a significant part in our system of justice'. Of course the operative word here is 'significant'. What should it be taken to mean? Throughout this report we have taken it to mean that if there is to be change then it will be at the margin. Possibly the sort of modest increase nationally in the number of stipendiary magistrates which has taken place over the last 40 years. Were that to be the case, and assuming, as we calculated in Chapter Six, that one stipendiary currently accomplishes about the same amount of work as 30 lay magistrates (if lay tribunals are always assumed to comprise three magistrates), then a two-fold increase in the number of stipendiaries to 200 would mean that there would still be a need for in excess of 27,000 lay magistrates.

It follows that the courts will continue to have need of persons to train the lay magistrates, draw up their sitting rotas, take minutes at their bench meetings, organise their elections for bench chairman, and so on. Moreover, the lay magistrates will still need rooms in which to assemble and to which to retire. The point is this. Were there to be a step change in the use of lay magistrates then, over time, substantial savings would accrue. Over time there would be a need for fewer courtrooms and offices and this could be converted, when buildings came up for replacement, to fewer or smaller courthouses – an item prominent in the courts' budget. It follows that there are both marginal and step-change, short-term and long-term, considerations at issue.

Further issues to be considered are:

- the degree to which justice should continue to be dispensed locally (see Chapter One)
- the degree to which the magistrates' courts should continue to be administered locally and separate from the Crown Court.

A busy urban court centre which combined an upper and lower tier court and which, in addition to the use of lay magistrates, flexibly employed professional judges in whatever cases were considered to require their expertise, would likely accrue greater cost advantages than the substitution of stipendiaries for lay magistrates in a little populated low crime rural area covered by several relatively little-used lower tier courthouses. These policy issues self-evidently lie beyond our scope and competence, but they illustrate how limited are cost estimates of the sort arrived at in Chapter Six.

Finally, reference must be made to the cost implications that lie beyond the Magistrates' Courts Service of employing different types of magistrates. There is first the question of the opportunity costs of employing lay magistrates. The majority (three-fifths) of lay magistrates are actively employed in the labour market. Were lay magistrates more representative of the community at large the proportion would be higher. They are not a free service. Many of them are employed in the public sector. While they are in court their services are lost to business, the education or health services, and so on.

Just as difficult is the question of the knock-on costs for other criminal justice agencies of using stipendiary magistrates. Our evidence indicates that, were there to be a doubling of the number of stipendiaries, then the number of court appearances per case would reduce by 10,270. We estimate that this is achieved at a cost of £0.88 million if all the attributable costs are considered.

It is also the case that, were the existing pattern of stipendiary decision-making to continue, then there would be a significantly larger prison population, probably with regard to the remand population and certainly with regard to the sentenced population. That would represent a very substantial additional cost for the penal system. We estimate that doubling the number of stipendiaries would increase the number of remands in custody by around 6,200 per annum at a cost of around £24 million. Under the same assumptions, the number of custodial sentences would increase by 2,760. This represents a cost, primarily on HM Prison Service, of £13.6 million. This can in part be offset by taking into account the type of sentence that the custodial sentence is replacing. If this would typically be a community penalty, then the overall cost increase would be around £8.5 million.

However, quite apart from the difficulties we have encountered estimating what the likely increase in the prison population might be, it does not necessarily follow that, were there to be an increased number of stipendiary magistrates, their sentencing policies would replicate those of stipendiaries today. The sentencing policies of the courts ultimately reduce to the political decisions of the government and parliament.

It makes no sense treating an existing decision-making pattern as if, like the weather coming in from the Atlantic, it represents a fate about which nothing can be done. By the same token, if lay magistrates combined with their legal advisors fail, to take one example highlighted above, to challenge the time-wasting applications of the prosecution or defence, that also is something about which a good deal can be done. Many of the differences revealed in this study are understandable, but they are not immutable. The issues and problems we have highlighted could be addressed through different initiatives: they do not suggest that a particular change in the balance of the lay and stipendiary magistracy is the only solution but they point to ways in which more effective practices could be adopted.

8.7 PUBLIC PERCEPTIONS OF THE DIFFERENCES BETWEEN GROUPS OF MAGISTRATES

We end this report where we began: with references to the public at large and the suggestion that the lay magistracy represents an aspect of participatory democracy. In Chapter Seven it emerged from our brief survey of other jurisdictions that there is no straightforward relationship between the degree to which the idea of democracy is embedded in a nation and the involvement by lay persons in judicial decision-making. The criminal court systems of some well-established democracies involve lay persons, others do not. There are also many different ways in which lay persons can be and are involved. Further, because criminal court arrangements are cultural and historical products they are not easily transferable. It is instructive to see what is done elsewhere, but comparative analysis does not provide an answer to the question of what should be done. It was for this reason that we were asked to investigate, by means of a survey, how much the public knows about our magistrates' courts and what value, if any, it attaches to one type of magistrate or means of arriving at decisions or another.

It is clear that the differences between lay and stipendiary magistrates and the manner in which they work are not widely understood. Whereas the overwhelming majority of members of the public have heard of magistrates' courts and the office of magistrate, almost three-quarters are unaware of the difference between lay and stipendiary magistrates. A clear majority knows that most cases begin and end in the magistrates' court and bare majorities know that there is no jury in magistrates' courts and that most magistrates, though trained, are not legally-qualified. But only a minority are aware of roughly how frequently lay magistrates sit in court. This general lack of awareness, which not surprisingly varies somewhat according to experience of attending court, social status and education, does not mean, however, that members of the public do not have views, when the question is raised, about what sort of tribunal should deal with different types of cases. It would be a mistake to construe lack of public knowledge with lack of opinion or public indifference.

When asked whether particular types of cases are better dealt with by a single magistrate or by a panel of magistrates, the majority of members of the public think that serious issues – the question of guilt in contested cases and whether someone should be sentenced to imprisonment, for example – should be decided by panels. These views are most likely to be held by the best educated and well informed members of the public. By contrast, most respondents think that less serious matters normally dealt by way of a fine – summary motoring offences, for example – are suitable to be dealt with by a single magistrate.

When the characteristics of lay and stipendiary magistrates are explained to the public, and in the survey we conducted they were explained, most people say that there is a role for both lay and stipendiary magistrates. Very few people, however, think that what is currently the case – lay magistrates dealing with the overwhelming majority of the business – should be the case. They favour the work being divided evenly, or think the balance does not greatly matter.

8.8   CONCLUDING COMMENT

Our findings are not entirely consistent nor are their implications entirely clear. It is nevertheless possible to anticipate likely public reactions to certain suggestions for change, were they to be widely canvassed. The office of Justice of the Peace is ancient. It represents an important tradition of voluntary public service for which, despite some recruitment difficulties in some parts of the country, thousands of candidates continue to come forward, prepared to give up a great deal of their time for no financial reward. In no other jurisdiction of which we are aware does the criminal court system depend so heavily on such voluntary unpaid effort. At no stage during the fieldwork of which this report is the product has it been suggested to us that in most respects the magistrates' courts do not work well or fail to command general confidence. Successive governments, moreover, have favoured the encouragement of *active citizens* or of an *active community*. The lay magistracy, whatever its imperfections, is a manifestation of those concepts. We doubt that any suggestion that the role of Justice of the Peace in the magistrates' courts be eliminated or greatly diminished would be widely understood or supported.

It is also evident, however, that the public does not have strong feelings about the precise role of lay magistrates in the magistrates' courts. They think that summary offences, particularly if not contested, are suitable to be dealt with by a single magistrate. They equally consider that more serious decisions should be taken not by single persons but by panels. Cost considerations, as well as tradition, suggest that that could only be done, in the short-term at least, by continuing to make extensive use of lay magistrates. Criminal justice practitioners, though appreciative that most lay magistrates deliver a quality service, have greater confidence in professional judges. Successive governments have introduced initiatives to make the criminal courts more efficient, not least to reduce the time that cases take to complete. Stipendiary magistrates, not surprisingly, are more efficient and inquisitorial in their approach. However, this has to be balanced against the potential increase in cost to the Prison Service of their decisions.

These wider considerations suggest that the nature and balance of the contribution made by lay and stipendiary magistrates could be altered so as better to satisfy these different considerations without prejudicing the integrity of a system founded on strong traditions and widely supported.

Appendix A

Figure A.1

Age of lay magistrates within the ten sampled courts

	Up to 30	30-39	40-49	50-54	55-59	60-65	66-69	Total
Rural 1	-	2	7	11	11	16	3	50
	-	4%	14%	22%	22%	32%	6%	100%
Rural 2	-	3	15	21	29	9	7	84
	-	4%	18%	25%	35%	11%	8%	100%
Mixed Urban-Rural	-	-	11	15	18	22	12	78
	-	-	14%	19%	23%	28%	15%	100%
Urban 1	-	4	15	25	35	29	11	119
	-	3%	13%	21%	29%	24%	9%	100%
Urban 2	-	3	29	31	52	40	25	180
	-	2%	16%	17%	29%	22%	14%	100%
Urban 3	-	16	67	70	79	121	67	420
	-	4%	16%	17%	19%	29%	16%	100%
Metropolitan 1	1	30	83	67	57	65	43	346
	*%	9%	24%	19%	16%	19%	12%	100%
Metropolitan 2	-	25	68	66	65	67	29	320
	-	8%	21%	21%	20%	21%	9%	100%
Outer London	-	14	31	34	26	21	14	140
	-	10%	22%	24%	19%	15%	10%	100%
Inner London	-	6	10	12	11	15	8	62
	-	10%	16%	19%	18%	24%	13%	100%
Total	1	103	336	352	383	405	219	1,799
	*%	6%	19%	20%	21%	22%	12%	100%

Source: Justices' Clerks' Records
* = <0.5%

Figure A.2

Ethnicity: lay magistrates and population generally

	White	Black Caribbean, Black African, Black other	Indian, Pakistani, Bangladeshi Chinese	Other	Not known	Total
Magistrates England and Wales Number Percentage	21,950 85%	430 2%	541 2%	186 1%	2,825 11%	25,932[1] 100%
General population for England and Wales (1991 census)	94%	2%	3%	1%	-	100%

[1] Figures exclude Magistrates in the Duchy of Lancaster

Figure A.3

Occupation profile of lay magistrates locally

PSA	Lecturers and Teachers	Civil Servants	Local Government employees	Farmers and other agricultural workers	Healthcare Profess-ionals e.g. doctors/ nurses	Other health workers	Other Professional e.g. Acc/Surv	Employees of National Companies	Employees of Local Companies/ Orgs	Employees of Charitable Orgs.	Self Employed	Not in paid employ-ment / Retired	Total
Rural 1	2	2	5	1	2	1	1	4	8	-	5	20	51
	4%	4%	10%	2%	4%	2%	2%	8%	16%	-	10%	39%	100%
Rural 2	4	-	9	6	4	-	15	-	17	-	-	26	81
	5%	-	11%	7%	5%	-	19%	-	21%	-	-	32%	100%
Mix Urb/Rural	5	3	4	-	1	4	4	7	4	1	11	29	73
	7%	4%	5%	-	1%	5%	5%	10%	5%	-	15%	40%	100%
Urban 2	12	6	7	-	6	3	17	14	7	-	26	36	134
	9%	4%	5%	-	4%	2%	13%	10%	5%	-	19%	27%	100%
Urban 3	25	9	29	2	25	7	42	32	50	-	48	163	432
	6%	2%	7%	*%	6%	2%	10%	7%	12%	-	11%	38%	100%
Metropoln 1	42	13	22	-	35	25	43	49	27	-	66	20	342
	12%	4%	6%	-	10%	7%	13%	14%	8%	-	19%	6%	100%
Metropoln 2	36	16	16	-	27	5	19	27	50	-	43	81	320
	11%	5%	5%	-	8%	2%	6%	8%	16%	-	13%	25%	100%
Inner London	2	2	17	-	10	6	1	3	8	-	1	12	62
	3%	3%	27%	-	16%	10%	2%	5%	13%	-	2%	19%	100%
Total	128	51	109	9	110	51	142	136	171	1	200	387	1495
	9%	3%	7%	1%	7%	3%	9%	9%	11%	*%	13%	26%	100%

Source: LCD records held centrally
Court Data for courts Urban 1 and Outer London were unavailable
* = <0.5%

Figure A.4

Lay magistrates: ideal number of court sittings per annum

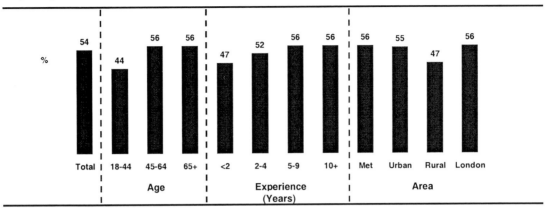

Base: All lay magistrates (1,120)
Source: Magistrates' Questionnaire

Figure A.5

Magistrates' views on whether there should be a maximum number of sittings

	Stipe	Lay Magistrates						
	Total	Total	Court area type			Age		
			London	Urban	Rural	Under 44	45-64	65+
Base: All Respondents	27	1,120	126	832	162	123	814	173
	%	%	%	%	%	%	%	%
Yes - Adult courts	78	71	63	72	75	68	70	76
Yes - All jurisdictions	78	79	77	78	84	75	79	80

Source: Magistrates' questionnaire

Figure A.6

Magistrates' views on what the upper limit for sittings should be

	Stipe	Lay Magistrates						
	Total	Total	Court area type			Age		
			London	Urban	Rural	Under 44	45-64	65+
Base: All who think there should be an upper limit for adult courts	21	807	80	604	123	84	583	132
Adult courts (average number of sittings)	61	77	78	79	58	90	76	70
Base: All who think there should be an upper limit for all jurisdictions	21	885	97	651	137	92	648	138
All jurisdictions (average number of sittings)	66	97	112	99	70	104	99	88

Source: Magistrates' questionnaire

Figure A.7

Court sessions observed

	Unweighted		Weighted[1]	
Total	535	100%	535	100%
Bench characteristics:		%		%
Lay	402	75	430	80
Stipe	130	24	98	18
Mixed	3	1	6	1
Court:				
Rural 1	40	7	13	2
Rural 2	52	10	9	2
Mixed Urban-Rural	43	8	16	3
Urban 1	50	9	30	6
Urban 2	53	10	36	7
Urban 3	70	13	95	18
Metropolitan 1	60	11	119	22
Metropolitan 2	57	11	119	22
Outer London	57	11	37	7
Inner London	53	10	63	12

Source: Observation data

[1] Weights were applied to make the data representative of the actual number of sessions in the 10 courts in the observation period (see figure B.1 in appendix B).

Figure A.8

Appearance type of observed sessions – bench characteristics

	Total	Lay	Stipe	Mixed
Weighted base: All appearances	4,717	3,620	1,090	35
	%	%	%	%
Crime	83	83	81	94
Summary motoring	11	10	12	--
Licensing	*	*	--	--
Fine default	1	1	1	--
Non-criminal Youth Court	*	*	--	--
Other	6	6	6	6

Source: Observation data

-- = 0%

* = <0.5%

Figure A.9

Appearance type of observed sessions

	Total	Rural 1	Rural 2	Mixed Urban -rural	Urban 1	Urban 2	Urban 3	Metro-politan 1	Metro-politan 2	Outer London	Inner London
Weighted base: all appearances	4,717	65	82	214	253	246	806	1,170	1,137	321	424
	%	%	%	%	%	%	%	%	%	%	%
Crime	83	74	76	81	76	75	94	88	72	76	92
Summary motoring	11	18	20	16	12	13	4	3	20	16	7
Licensing	*	5	1	1	*	1	--	--	*	*	*
Fine default	1	3	1	--	*	4	1	1	*	1	*
Non-criminal Youth Court	*	--	--	--	--	--	--	*	*	--	--
Other	6	2	2	2	12	7	1	8	7	7	1

Source: Observation data

* = <0.5%

-- = 0%

Figure A.10
Profile of offences observed across the ten courts

	Lay	Stipe
Base: All defendants in criminal appearances	2,690 %	1,161 %
Theft and handling	25	25
Violence	21	17
Burglary	8	7
Criminal damage	6	4
Drugs	6	6
Robbery	3	3
Sex	2	3
Deception / fraud / forgery	2	2
Other indictable	6	7
Motoring (non-summary)	6	7
Breach of court order	5	3
Summary non-motoring	2	3
Private prosecution	*	3
Other	5	8
Not stated	3	2

Source: Observation data

* = <0.5%

Figure A.11

Social grade definitions

Social grade	Social Status	Occupation
A	Upper middle class	Higher managerial, administrative or professional
B	Middle class	Intermediate managerial, administrative or professional
C1	Lower middle class	Supervisory or clerical and junior managerial, administrative or professional
C2	Skilled working class	Skilled manual workers
D	Working class	Semi and unskilled manual workers
E	Those at the lowest level of subsistence	State pensioners or widows (no other earner), casual or lowest grade workers

These are the standard social grade classifications using definitions agreed between IPSOS-RSL and NRS

Source: National Readership Survey (NRS Ltd) July 1997 to June 1998.

APPENDIX B

Copies of data collection instruments for B1 to B5 are available from
Crime and Criminal Justice Unit
Research Development and Statistics Directorate
Tel. 020 7273 3807

B1   OBSERVATION DATA

Court observation took place between April and June 2000 in the ten courts sampled.

The aim was to observe 600 court sessions (60 in each of the ten courts sampled) across a variety of sessions.

Observers did not go to courts dealing solely with summary motoring, council tax evasion, licensing, civil cases, Early Administration Hearings etc. However, in some courts where there was a mix of business, these types of appearances occurred. In this instance the observers simply recorded the number of appearances that were dealt with by the magistrate (including those where the defendant was not present) and the time at which they finished dealing with those appearances.

Courts where there was a trial taking place could have been selected, but we asked that these were in the minority. In total, we aimed to only record information on 18 trials in each court. We tried to cover sessions dealing with two or three trials and asked observers to allocate around one-tenth of their sessions to trials. Observers were asked to avoid trials that were likely to take longer than a day.

Observers working in an area where there was not a full-time stipendiary magistrate were asked to give precedence to sessions that were being chaired by a (part-time or visiting) stipendiary magistrate (unless it featured a trial that was likely to go on beyond the day being observed).

For each session, details were recorded on the following:

- start and end time
- type of court
- specialisation of court
- tribunal composition.

For each appearance within the session, details were recorded on the following:

- start and end times
- type of prosecutor
- type of appearance
- retirement details
- defendant details
- offence details
- type of hearing
- principal decisions made
- bail/ custody decisions
- adjournment details
- details of sentences passed
- role of clerk and magistrate
- magistrate's manner.

Adult Courts and Youth Courts were observed. We aimed for around one-quarter of the sessions to relate to Youth Courts, however in some of the less busy locations there were not enough Youth Court sittings to make this possible. In these cases we asked observers to give priority to the Youth Courts to ensure we had enough observations.

Sixteen observers were recruited to carry out court observation and collate the data from the ten courts sampled. In relation to the specification of the individual, we were looking for people who had:

- previous research experience
- reasonable knowledge of the workings of a magistrates' court – so they understood key parts of the process
- some knowledge of the law as observers were expected to categorise cases by type of crime
- not had direct experience of working in the magistrates' court in which we asked them to observe – any contact they might have had with the court could compromise their judgements
- were able to give us 15 days work (probably 30 half-days) in the period April – June 2000 (following a four day training session in March)
- some experience of working with computers
- a suitable home telephone connection point for a CAPI machine modem.

After recruitment, the observers undertook a four day training session in March 2000 and were trained to look at many aspects of the court proceedings and to use the computer technology used to record the data.

All observers took part in a minimum of two live practice sessions at their allocated courts to become used to the data collection equipment and the complexities of the information they were being asked to collect. Feedback to the research team at the end of the practice sessions enabled the recording instruments to be refined.

Prior to the observers sitting in court, a meeting was held with members of the team from Bristol University, RSGB and the magistrates' courts' clerks from each of the ten courts involved. The data collection exercise was explained and their permission to observe the courts was requested.

Observers introduced themselves before working in the court, and always carried identification explaining who they were.

Pen technology was used to record the data. The pen interface allows answers to be recorded either by touching the screen in the appropriate place with an electronic pen or by writing in answers in the space allocated on the screen. This feature allowed observers to record information quickly, quietly and accurately, being as unobtrusive as possible.

Data was managed daily as follows:

- assignments were allocated to interviewers according to which courts they were sitting in
- progress was monitored on a daily basis, and all data was transferred back to the office daily
- observer behaviour was tracked in terms of days worked, sessions observed, hours worked and time and length of interview. This allowed assistance to be offered to those interviewers who were experiencing any difficulties
- daily updates were received on answers to pre-coded questions
- a free phone help line number was available for observers, for any technical problems they were having with the equipment, or any queries they had.

A total of 535 sessions and 5,048 appearances/ events were observed. The analysis here is based on 3,874 criminal appearances. Excluded are summary motoring appearances, licensing matters, fine defaults, non-criminal Youth Court appearances and breaks in proceedings.

On completion of the data collection, the data were edited and weighted. Weights were applied as set out on Figure B.1 to ensure the sample was representative of the number of adult and youth sessions within each court.

Figure B.1

Weighting matrix, observation data

Total number of sessions during the observation period

	Rural 1		Rural 2		Mixed urban-rural		Urban 1		Urban 2		Urban 3		Metropol 1		Metropol 2		Outer London		Inner London		Total
	Lay	Stipe	Lay	Stipe	Lay	Stipe	Lay	Stipe	Lay	Stipe	Lay	Stipe	Lay	Stipe	Lay	Stipe	Lay	Stipe	Lay	Stipe	
Adult	84	0	56	2	102	13	197	12	248	0	481	83	552	186	658	123	182	44	132	203	3,358
Youth	14	0	10	0	7	0	24	0	31	0	170	5	184	5	129	14	54	6	96	56	805
																					4,163

Proportion of the total number of sessions during the observation period

	Rural 1		Rural 2		Mixed urban-rural		Urban 1		Urban 2		Urban 3		Metropol 1		Metropol 2		Outer London		Inner London		Total
	Lay	Stipe	Lay	Stipe	Lay	Stipe	Lay	Stipe	Lay	Stipe	Lay	Stipe	Lay	Stipe	Lay	Stipe	Lay	Stipe	Lay	Stipe	
Adult	0.020	0	0.013	0	0.025	0.003	0.047	0.003	0.060	0	0.116	0.020	0.133	0.045	0.158	0.030	0.044	0.011	0.032	0.049	0.807
Youth	0.003	0	0.002	0	0.002	0	0.005	0	0.007	0	0.041	0.001	0.044	0.001	0.031	0.003	0.013	0.001	0.023	0.013	0.193
Total	0.023	0	0.015	0	0.027	0.003	0.052	0.003	0.067	0	0.157	0.021	0.177	0.046	0.189	0.033	0.057	0.012	0.055	0.062	1.000

Source: Courts' clerks' records for the period during which the observations were conducted

B2   COURT USERS' SURVEY

A sample of 400 regular court users was interviewed. Respondents were interviewed by telephone at home or at work at a time convenient to them using computer-assisted telephone interviewing (CATI) technology. The back-checking procedures which were carried out met the requirements of the Market Research Interviewer Quality Control Scheme (IQCS).

People working in the ten participating courts sampled were approached by the court observers and asked whether they would be willing to take part in the study. If they agreed they were given a letter explaining a little about the study and the purpose of the interview. They were assured that all information and views collected (including their own identities as well as those of the participating courts) would remain entirely confidential. Names, telephone numbers and details of when would be the most convenient time to ring were collected and supplied to the telephone centre.

The court observers were instructed to recruit approximately equal numbers of names of persons in five categories: court personnel (legal advisors and ushers); prosecutors (mostly CPS personnel but including Television Licensing Authority, Inland Revenue and other prosecuting officials); police officers and other professional witnesses; defence lawyers; probation officers, social workers and Victim Support co-ordinators.

Subsequent to the initial contacts it was made known to the research team that there was within the CPS a research access protocol to be satisfied centrally. CPS headquarters was contacted by the University of Bristol and following explanations about the nature of the project approval was transmitted by headquarters to local Chief Crown Prosecutors for local CPS personnel to participate.

From the original list of approximately 600 names, 400 regular court users were interviewed. The profile of these is presented in Figure B.2.

The interview took 17 minutes to administer.

The interviews took place during May 2000. The data were analysed by sub-groups (age, sex, ethnicity, court role, experience of magistrates by type of magistrate, frequency of court attendances, duration of experience attending magistrates' courts, and so on).

Figure B.2 provides details of the sample achieved.

Figure B.2

Court role, by court

	Total	Rural 1	Rural 2	Mixed urban-rural	Urban 1	Urban 2	Urban 3	Prov Met 1	Prov Met 2	Outer London	Inner London
Clerk	47	3	3	-	3	6	10	7	8	6	1
Solicitor	115	14	11	14	8	1	20	8	18	10	11
Barrister	30	1	1	1	3	-	8	6	1	7	2
Police officer	52	7	4	5	7	2	8	1	2	15	1
Probation officer	36	2	1	3	4	7	9	2	3	2	3
CPS prosecutor	43	6	2	1	7	3	8	4	6	4	2
Victim support worker	5	-	-	1	-	1	-	-	3	-	-
Social services social worker	15	3	1	-	1	3	1	2	3	1	-
Usher	35	2	5	-	1	3	10	3	4	5	2
Other	23	2	-	-	2	2	4	4	2	6	1

Base: All court users (400)

The data are reported unweighted as the researchers had no information on the relative balance of the groups present in the participating courts across all sessions.

B3 MAGISTRATES' DIARIES

All magistrates from the ten courts selected for the study were invited to complete two consecutive three-week diaries.

The method by which diaries were sent to the magistrates varied by court. In some cases diaries were sent directly to the magistrates from RSGB's offices. In other cases the courts agreed to act as intermediaries.

The diaries were completed between 27 March and 6 May 2000. The six week diary period includes Easter week and the May Bank Holiday.

Diaries were sent to 1,916 lay magistrates of whom 1,151 (60%) returned at least one diary. 868 (45%) returned both diaries. In total, of the 3,832 diaries sent out, 2,019 (53%) were returned.

The data for lay magistrates were weighted so that the number of magistrates returning at least one diary for each court was in proportion to the number of lay magistrates sitting at each court at the time of the survey.

Of the stipendiary magistrates, all those who sat in the selected courts were eligible for the research. Forty-nine three-week diaries were returned from the 74 that were sent out.

The stipendiary magistrates' diary data are reported unweighted. The stipendiary magistrates' diary data were analysed by all stipendiaries (full-time and part-time) and by full time stipendiaries.

Where magistrates had returned diaries saying that they had not undertaken any activities within the period then these were included in the analysis. The only diaries excluded were those returned from people who said that they had ceased their duties as a magistrate.

B4 MAGISTRATES' QUESTIONNAIRES

All magistrates from the ten courts selected for the study were invited to complete a self-completion questionnaire, as well as two consecutive three-week diaries.

The method by which questionnaires were sent to the magistrates varied by courts. In some cases they were sent directly to the magistrates from RSGB's offices. In other cases the courts agreed to act as intermediaries.

The questionnaires were sent out on 6 March. The last day for return was 24 May.

Questionnaires were sent to 1,916 lay magistrates of whom 1,120 (58%) completed and returned one by the closing date.

The data for lay magistrates were weighted so that the number of magistrates returning a questionnaire was in proportion to the number of lay magistrates sitting at each court at the time of the survey.

The court profile of the magistrates across the ten courts who responded to the survey is shown in Figure B.3 together with the profile by court of the numbers of lay magistrates we were informed were current magistrates at the time of the research. This second figure equated to the number of questionnaires we despatched for each court.

The responses show a relatively poor return from Metropolitan 1 (19% of issued profile, 12% of returned profile) and a relatively good response from Metropolitan 2 (17% of issued profile, 20% of returned profile).

Figure B.3

Profile of the magistrates who returned questionnaires compared to that for all lay magistrates across the ten courts

	Questionnaires despatched	Magistrates returning questionnaires
Base: All magistrates in the ten sample courts	1,916	1,120
	%	%
Rural 1	3	4
Rural 2	4	5
Mixed urban-rural	4	5
Urban 1	6	7
Urban 2	9	10
Urban 3	25	25
Metropolitan 1	19	12
Metropolitan 2	17	20
Outer London	7	7
Inner London	6	5

Of the stipendiary magistrates, all those who sat in the selected courts were eligible for the research. Twenty-seven questionnaires were returned from the 37 that were sent out: a response rate of 73%.

The stipendiary magistrate questionnaire data are reported unweighted.

A helpline was provided in case magistrates wished to clarify any of the questions.

B5   PUBLIC OPINION SURVEY

A sample of 1,753 adults across England and Wales were interviewed by means of RSGB's Omnibus survey. The Omnibus survey goes out to 2,000 respondents every week, asking a variety of questions from different sources.

A representative sample was achieved of 1,753 adults, aged 16 or more in England and Wales. Respondents were selected from a minimum of 100 sampling points by a random location method especially developed for the RSGB omnibus survey.

A unique sampling system has been developed by Taylor Nelson Sofres for its own use. Utilising 1991 UK Census small area statistics and the Post Office Address File (PAF), the eligible area of the country has been divided into 600 areas of equal population. The areas within each Standard Region were stratified into population density bands, and within band in descending order by percentage of population in socio-economic Grade's I and II.

To maximise the statistical accuracy of Omnibus sampling, sequential waves of fieldwork are allocated systematically across the sampling frame so as to ensure maximum geographical dispersion. The 600 primary sampling units are allocated to 25 sub-samples of 24 points each, with each sub-sample in itself being a representative drawing from the frame. For each wave of Omnibus fieldwork a set of sub-samples is selected so as to provide the number of sample points required (typically c. 130 for 2,000 interviews). Across sequential waves of fieldwork all sub-samples are systematically worked, thereby reducing the clustering effects on questionnaires asked for two or more consecutive weeks.

Each primary sampling unit is divided into two geographically distinct segments, each containing as far as possible, equal populations. The segments comprise aggregations of complete postcode sectors. Within each half (known as the A and B halves) postcode sectors have been sorted by the percentage of the population in socio-economic groups I and II. One postcode sector from each primary sampling unit is selected for each Omnibus, alternating on successive selections between the A and B halves of the primary sampling unit, again to reduce clustering effects.

For each wave of interviewing each interviewer is supplied with two blocks of 100 addresses, drawn from different parts of the sector. Addresses are contacted systematically with three doors being left after each successful interview.

Interviewing is restricted to after 2 p.m. on weekdays or all day at the weekend. To ensure a balanced sample of adults within effective contacted addresses, a quota is set by sex (male, female, housewife, female non-housewife); within female housewife, presence of children and working status and within men, working status.

The interviews took place during the period 14 to 18 June 2000. Respondents were interviewed at home using computer-assisted personal interviewing (CAPI) pen technology.

Interviewers were organised by SFR's regional managers according to RSGB's detailed instructions about the survey and administration procedures. The back-checking procedures which were carried out met the requirements of the Market Research Interviewer Quality Control Scheme (IQCS).

After coding and editing the data, weights were used to allow for sampling variation. The weighting matrix can be supplied on request.

B6   SURVEYING OTHER JURISDICTIONS

In May 2000 the Directorate of Legal Affairs of the Council of Europe in Strasbourg sent out, at the request of the research team, to the Heads of Delegation of the 41 member states the following inquiry:

> Do lay persons – that is non-law qualified persons (whether part-time or full-time, ad hoc or long-term appointed, voluntary or unpaid) – play any part in criminal court decision making as finders of fact or sentencers?
>
> To the extent that lay persons are involved, is this a longstanding arrangement or a recent development? And to the extent that lay persons are not involved, used they to be?
>
> For each category of lay person involved, how are the lay persons recruited and appointed, what is their tenure of office, to what degree are they trained, and are they financially compensated for their services (with either salaries, loss of earnings or expenses)? Further, to what extent are lay persons representative of the community at large?

At the time of writing (November 2000) 23 member states had replied to the inquiry. In addition to the survey of Council of Europe member states, ad hoc inquiries were made to other countries, mainly Commonwealth countries, known originally to have used lay magistrates or to continue to do so.

REFERENCES

Abraham H.J. (1993) *The Judicial Process* New York: Oxford University Press.

Active Community Unit (1999) *Giving Time, Getting Involved: A strategy Report by the Working Group on the Active Community*, London: Home Office Active Community Unit.

Ashworth A. (1998) *The Criminal Justice Process: an evaluative study*, 2nd Ed, Oxford: Oxford University Press.

Baldwin J. (1975) 'The Social Composition of the Magistracy', *British Journal of Criminology*, 171-4.

Bankowski Z.K., Hutton N.R. and McManus J.J. (1987) *Lay Justice*, Edinburgh: T.T.Clark.

Brookbanks W. (1998) 'Community Magistrates', *Law Talk*, 507, 5 October.

Burney (1979) *Magistrate, Court and Community*, London: Hutchinson.

Charman E., Gibson B., Honess T. and Morgan R. (1996) *Fine Impositions and Enforcement Following the Criminal Justice Act 1993,* Research Findings No. 36, London: Home Office Research and Statistics Directorate.

Criminal Justice Consultative Council (2000) *CCJC Newsletter,* Issue 18, Liverpool: Home Office.

Darbyshire P. (1997a) 'An Essay on the Importance and Neglect of the Magistracy', *Criminal Law Review*, 627-43.

Darbyshire P. (1997b) 'For the New Lord Chancellor - Some Causes for Concern About Magistrates', *Criminal Law Review*, 861-74.

Darbyshire P. (1999) A Comment on the Powers of Magistrates' Clerks', *Criminal Law Review*, 377-386.

Dignan, J. and Whynne, A. (1997) 'A Microcosm of the Local Community? Reflections on the Composition of the Magistracy in a Petty Sessional Division in the North Midlands' *British Journal of Criminology* 37:184.

Doran S. and Glenn R. (2000) *Lay Involvement in Adjudication*, Research Report No 11, Review of Criminal Justice System in Northern Ireland, Belfast: Criminal Justice Review Group.

Ernst and Young (1999) *Reducing Delay in the Criminal Justice System: Evaluation of the Pilot Schemes*, London: Home Office.

Flood-Page C. and Mackie A. (1988) *Sentencing Practice: an examination of decisions in magistrates' courts and the Crown Court in the mid-1990s*, Home Office Research Study No. 125, London: HMSO.

Gibson B. (ed.)(1999) *Human Rights and the Courts: Bringing Justice Home*, Winchester: Waterside.

Godzinsky V-M. de and Ervasti K. (1999) *Laymen as Judges*, Helsinki: National Research Institute of Legal Policy.

Harries Richard (1999) *The Cost of Criminal Justice,* Home Office Research Findings No. 103. Home Office Research and Statistics Directorate 1999.

Hedderman C. and Moxon D. (1992) Magistrates' Court or Crown Court? Mode of Trial Decisions and Sentencing, London: HMSO.

Henham R. (1990) Sentencing Principles and Magistrates' Sentencing Behaviour, Avebury.

Her Majesty's Magistrates' Court Service Inspectorate (1999) *Information for Management: The Core Performance Measures (CPMs)*, April 1999, London: MCSI.

Home Affairs Committee (1996) *Judicial Appointments,* House of Commons Home Affairs Committee 1995-6, 3rd Report of, London: HMSO.

Home Office (Narey Report) (1997a) *Review of Delay in the Criminal Justice System: A Report*, London: Home Office.

Home Office (1997b) *No More Excuses – A New Approach to Tacking Youth Crime in England and Wales* Command Paper 3809, London: Home Office.

Home Office (2000a) *Criminal Statistics England and Wales*, Cm 4649, London: Home Office.

Home Office (2000b) *Prison Statistics England and Wales 1999*, Cm 4805, London: HMSO

Hood R. (1972) *Sentencing the Motoring Offender*, London: Heinemann.

Hough M. and Roberts J.(1998) *Attitudes to Punishment: Findings from the British Crime Survey*, Home Office Research Study No. 179, London: Home Office.

Huckelsby A. (1997) 'Court Culture: An Explanation of Variations in the Use of Bail by Magistrates' Courts', *Howard Journal*, 129.

Ivkovic K.S. (1997) 'Lay participation in Decision-Making: A Croatian Perspective on Mixed Tribunals', *The Howard Journal*, 36: 406-423.

Jones P. (1985) 'Remand Decisions at Magistrates' Courts', in Moxon D. (Ed) *Managing Criminal Justice,* London: HMSO.

King M. and May C. (1985) *Black Magistrates,* London: Cobden Trust.

Lord Chancellor's Department (1998) *Management Information System 1997: Indicators and Data*, London: LCD.

Mahoney S. (2000) *Time Intervals for Criminal Proceedings in Magistrates' Courts: February 2000*, Information Bulletin 3/2000, London: Lord Chancellor's Department.

Mattinson J. and Mirrlees-Black C. (2000) *Attitudes to Crime and Criminal Justice - Findings from the 1998 BCS*, Home Office Research Study No. 200. London: Home Office.

Milton F. (1967) *The English Magistracy*, London: Oxford University Press.

Moir E. (1969) *The Justice of the Peace*, Harmondsworth: Penguin.

National Audit Office (1999) *Criminal Justice: Working Together*, HC 29, London: NAO.

Pateman C. (1970) *Participation and Democratic Theory*, London: Cambridge University Press.

Raine J.W. (1989) *Local Justice: Ideals and Reality*, Edinburgh: T&T Clark.

Richardson A. (1983) *Participation*, London: Routledge.

Riley D. and Vennard J. (1988) *Triable-Either-Way Cases: Crown Court or Magistrates' Court?*, Home Office Research Study 98, London: HMSO.

Royal Commission (1948) *Royal Commission on Justices of the Peace: Report,* Cmnd. 1191, London: HMSO.

Royal Commission (Runciman Report) (1993) *The Royal Commission on Criminal Justice: Report*, Cm 2263, London: HMSO
HMSO.

Seago P., Walker C. and Wall D. (1995) *The Role and Appointment of Stipendiary Magistrates*, Leeds: Centre of Criminal Justice Studies, University of Leeds.

Seago P., Walker C. and Wall D. (2000) 'The Development of the Professional Magistracy in England and Wales', *Criminal Law Review*, 631-651.

Seekings J. and Murray C. (1998) *Lay Assessors in South Africa's Magistrates' Courts*, Cape Town: University of Cape Town Law, Race and Gender Research Unit.

Skyrme, Sir T. (1994) *History of the Justices of the Peace*, Chichester: Barry Rose.

Tarling R. (1979) *Sentencing Practice in Magistrates' Courts*, Home Office Research Study No 56, London: HMSO.

Vennard J. (1981) *Contested Trials in Magistrates' Courts*, Home Office Research Study No 71, London: HMSO.

Vennard J. (1985) 'The Outcome of Contested Trials' in Moxon D. (ed) *Managing Criminal Justice*, London: Home Office.